Press De Vinne, Charles William Larned, Edward F Miner

History of the Battle Monument at West Point

Press De Vinne, Charles William Larned, Edward F Miner

History of the Battle Monument at West Point

ISBN/EAN: 9783337328221

Printed in Europe, USA, Canada, Australia, Japan

Cover: Foto ©ninafisch / pixelio.de

More available books at **www.hansebooks.com**

CONTENTS

	PAGE
History of the Battle Monument	1
Dedication of Site on Trophy Point	19
Prayers	23
Oration by General George B. McClellan	29
Dedication Ceremonies at West Point	83
Prayers	87
Address of General Wilson	89
Address of General Schofield	95
Address of Secretary of War	99
Address of Justice Brewer	103
Epilogue	113
List of Officers and Men Borne upon the Monument	117
Description of the Quarrying, Working, Transportation and Erection of the Battle Monument	221
Report of the Treasurer	239

LIST OF ILLUSTRATIONS

I Monument. *View from West* .	*Frontispiece*
II Monument. *Front view*. . .	*Facing page*	1
III Competitive Design of Babb, Cook & Willard	" "	67
IV Competitive Design of Carrere & Hastings .	" "	71
V Alternative Design of Carrere & Hastings .	" "	73
VI Competitive Design of R. W. Emerson .	" "	75
VII Grand Stand from the West . . .	" "	83
VIII Rostrum	" "	89
IX Grand Stand from the South . .	" "	103
X Fame. *View from West* . .	" "	113
XI Fame. *View from East*. . .	" "	117
XII Cylindrical Base, bearing Names of Officers	" "	119
XIII Sphere and Plinth, bearing names of Enlisted Men	" "	131
XIV Shaft in the Quarry .	" "	221

XV	Preparing the Shaft for Working	*Facing page* 225
XVI	Mounted on Journals for Cutting	" " 227
XVII	Mechanical Appliances for Polishing	" " 228
XVIII	On the Cars for Transportation	" " 231
XIX	From Station to Site	" " 232
XX	On the Way	" " 233
XXI	Arrival at Site	" " 234
XXII	Erection	" " 237

THE BATTLE MONUMENT
AT WEST POINT

THE polished monolith of granite that faces on the terre-plein of West Point the gateway of the Hudson Highlands, guarding like a giant sentinel the memory of two thousand heroes of the mighty struggle for principle which freed a race and welded a nation, was dedicated to its sacred function on a day of mingled cloud mists and sunbursts—fit type of the dark years of battle and of the glory of the victory which it commemorates.

The band of men whose roll is to be read upon its tablets, and high above whose names winged Fame stands poised with trumpet and outstretched wreath, are the battle victims of that little army which stood at the beginning of the fight of 1861 for all the military art our country knew. Its monument rests to-day within the borders of the great Academy which for half a century had kept alive the tradition of military integrity, discipline, simplicity, and science which inspired these men, and through them the mighty hosts of heroic volunteers who offered their lives for principle and country.

This is a monument to the regular army of the United States, erected by brothers to brothers, not in an invidious or vaunting spirit, but with a just pride in the great work wrought by the soul that went forth from this army into the leaderless masses of noble men who left the walks of peace for the hard field of fight. The regular army is justified in this pride, and rightly glories in this rock-hewn witness to a work well and faithfully done, not only in this War of the Rebellion, but by these same men in exile, hardships and peril on remote frontiers amidst savage foes — the advance-guard of our civilization, the protectors of a land which they did not possess, and the promoters of a great industrial development whose fruit was not theirs. This memorial was not built by a grateful country, but by voluntary offerings from the hard-won pay of comrades in the field within hearing of the roar of battle, and in sight of the dead whose memory it preserves. Was ever shaft so reared before, or with a sentiment more modest, tender, and unselfish?

Those who have guarded the sacred trust confided to them, and whose honor and pleasure it has been to bring it to fruition, have labored to express in the finished work the dignity of the sentiment that gave it birth. The granite block, hewn from the mountain — single, upright, shining like the deeds to which it bears witness; the polished sphere, rounded like their lives and belted with enduring bronze; the simple inscription:

IN MEMORY
OF THE
OFFICERS AND MEN
OF THE
REGULAR ARMY OF THE UNITED STATES
WHO FELL IN BATTLE DURING THE
WAR OF THE REBELLION
THIS MONUMENT IS ERECTED BY THEIR
SURVIVING COMRADES

— these are all conceived in reverence, and intended to speak simply and directly the purpose of the givers and the merits of the dead. It is but right to add that the designer, Stanford White, and the sculptor, Frederick MacMonnies, have given a generous and enthusiastic labor to the work far beyond the value of any money recompense received, and in the true spirit of the artist and patriotic citizen.

* * * * * *

In response to a request from the Secretary of the Building Committee of the Battle Monument Association that he should narrate the circumstances which surrounded the initiative of the undertaking, Col. Hasbrouck wrote as follows:

Fort Monroe, Va., Nov. 6, 1897.

My dear Larned:

I returned to Fort Monroe last week from detached service on a board which has kept me busily occupied for about two months. I have been trying to recall the facts and incidents connected with the Battle Monument, and the action taken just after the conception of the project, which might avail you for your article. I find that my memory is unreliable about many things that have happened so long ago and I am sorry and afraid that my letter will not be of much use to you. The idea of the monument originated at West Point and the successful efforts to arouse interest and to raise the necessary funds were made by the officers permanently and temporarily on duty at the Academy. I was ordered to West Point for duty in September, 1863, while north on sick leave. At that time all the officers temporarily on duty had seen service in the field and many of them had been disabled by either wounds or sickness. All knew and appreciated the services of the regulars; and the merits and deeds of officers and men who had fallen were constantly recalled. These services were well known at the front, but received little recognition in the press, which, from local and State pride, made special effort to exploit the achievements of their own volunteers. We all thought the regulars were not receiving their just dues, and that their services should be better known and permanently commemorated. Soon after my arrival I suggested one night after dinner at the Mess a Monument at West Point which should have inscribed upon it a list of the battles and the names of all the officers and men of the Regular Army who had been killed or died of wounds received in action. The idea was well received and a notice for a meeting the next Saturday, a day when most of the officers could attend, was sent out. The meeting was attended by many officers. Lieut. (afterwards Captain) Charles C. Parsons, 4th Artillery, was especially interested and enthusiastic. He was a very able and earnest man, and I think the success of the effort in its initial stages was more due to him than to any other single individual. It is my recollection that he was made chairman of this meeting. He thought it important to secure as soon as possible the co-operation of all in the Regular Service, and urged that letters be promptly written to officers in the field and at other stations, asking for their views and aid. He sent for the necessary stationery, and many letters were written before the meeting broke up. A number of officers were there, but I cannot recall with certainty any except Parsons and Captain A. T. Smith, 8th Infantry, now Colonel of the 13th Infantry. In a short time so many favorable responses were received that a regular organization was formed, a treasurer appointed, and subscriptions asked for.

Sincerely yours,

H. C. HASBROUCK.

The minutes of the Association formed under the impulse of this suggestion of Lieutenant Hasbrouck give a clear account of the early stages of the undertaking which has recently culminated in the dedication of a Monument bearing the names of every officer and soldier in the Regular Army of the United States who fell in battle or died of wounds received in the War of the Rebellion.

The following extracts are selected as giving the most important acts of the committees having it in charge as well as the names of their individual members:

West Point, N. Y., Oct. 6, 1863.

At a meeting of officers convened at West Point, N. Y., Oct. 6, 1863, for the purpose hereafter designated, First Lieutenant W. A. Elderkin, 1st Artillery, U. S. Army, was called to the chair, after which the following resolution was unanimously adopted:

For the purpose of perpetuating the memory of those officers of the Regular Army who shall have fallen in action or died from wounds received in the field during the present war, it is

Resolved—That an organization be hereby effected, to consist of a President, a Treasurer, a Secretary, and an Executive Committee of eleven, including the above-named, who shall be empowered to solicit and receive subscriptions, as shall hereafter be determined, for the erection of a Monument at this post, upon which shall be inscribed the names, etc., of those who are embraced within the purpose of this resolution.

Whereupon the following officers were designated to constitute this organization:

President: Col. A. H. Bowman, U. S. Engineers, and Superintendent

Treasurer: Prof. A. E. Church, Military Academy

Secretary: First Lieut. C. C. Parsons, 4th Artillery, U. S. Army

Lieut.-Col. H. B. Clitz, Maj. 12th Infantry, U. S. A., and Comdt.

Capt. W. P. Chambliss, 5th Cavalry, U. S. Army

Capt. S. V. Benet, Ordnance

Capt. M. D. McAlister, Engineers

Capt. L. Lorain, 3d Artillery

First Lieut. A. T. Smith, 8th Infantry

First Lieut. W. A. Elderkin, 1st Artillery

First Lieut. H. B. Noble, 8th Infantry

Executive Committee.

And the chairman of the meeting, in conjunction with Lieut. Hasbrouck, 4th Artillery, and Captain Bradford, Ordnance Corps, was directed to notify these officers of their selection, and request their acceptance. On further motion, the

Executive Committee was directed to establish a pro rata standard of subscription, to fill vacancies among themselves, and to inquire into the expediency of obtaining permission from the Secretary of War to forward circulars, etc., through the Adjutant-General's Office.

On motion, the meeting adjourned to meet at Lieut. Hasbrouck's quarters on Friday evening following.

W. A. ELDERKIN,
First Lieut. 1st Artillery, U. S. Army,
President.

C. C. PARSONS,
First Lieut. 4th Artillery, U. S. Army,
Secretary.

West Point, N. Y., Oct. 9, 1863.

The meeting assembled, pursuant to adjournment, and resolved itself into the Executive Committee previously designated. Present — all the members except Col. Bowman, Prof. Church, and Capt. Chambliss. Lieut. Elderkin in the chair. The minutes of the last meeting were read, and on motion accepted, with the following amendment:

That the Superintendent of the Military Academy and Commandant of the Corps of Cadets should become ex-officio members of the Executive Committee, the former being also President.

On motion, the Committee adjourned to meet at the call of the Secretary.

Lieut. Elderkin, from Committee on Notification, reported that the officers selected to constitute the organization had been severally waited upon, with the exception of Captain Chambliss, absent from the post, and that each, with the above exception, had signified his acceptance.

Report adopted and Committee discharged.

On motion, the following Sub-committees were appointed:

Design and Execution.

Col. Bowman,   Lieut.-Col. Clitz,
Lieut. Elderkin.

Finance.

Prof. Church,   Capt. Benet,
Capt. McAlister.

Site.

Col. Bowman,   Capt. Chambliss,
Capt. Lorain.

Ceremonies.

Lieut.-Col. Clitz,   Lieut. Smith,
Lieut. Noble.

The following is the circular prepared by the Executive Committee:

West Point, N. Y., ...

Sir:

In response to what is believed to be the wish of all who have an interest in the subject, the Officers now stationed at West Point have effected an organization for the purpose of erecting at that post a Monument, to be called THE BATTLE MONUMENT, upon which shall be inscribed the names of all Officers of the Regular Army who, during the present war, shall have been killed or died of wounds received in the field.

It is not deemed necessary that any elaborate argument should set forth the propriety of earnest action in behalf of this object. It is an admitted fact, that while in other countries and other ages places are assigned in the historic mausoleum of the nation's illustrious dead, for those who have fallen for the public good, the soldiers of the American army are often permitted to rest among the unknown dead, while their names find no place in the annals of the stormy scenes in which, perhaps, they were the most exalted actors.

Is it not fit, therefore, that at West Point, the great central post around which cluster some of the richest associations of the Regular Army, to which would cheerfully resort all who wish to pay a tribute to the gallant dead,— under the shadow of the Academy which at last receives her sons and all who fight or fall beside them,— should be erected a Monument which shall supply the want that now exists?

To the dead it would offer the grateful homage of fraternal hearts,— to the living, still another inspiration to heroic virtues and sublime self-devotion.

The plan of action that is proposed has been carefully sought out, and it is trusted that, with a favorable response, a sufficient sum may be raised to make the *Battle Monument*, in design and durability, entirely worthy of its purpose.

It seems unnecessary that those who have undertaken to initiate this project should disavow any undue assumption in regard to it, since they earnestly ask from their brother officers, in the field or elsewhere, such instructions or suggestions as may tend to forward the purpose that is held in view.

For the purpose of indicating a standard of subscription, the following rates are proposed. Every one, however, will feel at liberty to offer a greater or less sum, as circumstances permit:

Maj.-General,	$27.00	Major, .	$10.00
Brig.-General, .	18.00	Captain, .	8.00
Colonel, .	13.00	Lieutenant, .	7.00
Lieut.-Colonel, .	11.00		

(Approximating to six per cent. of monthly pay, for one month.)

Beside your personal subscription, your co-operation with your associates in the field is also solicited, since this circular may not otherwise reach them on account of the difficulty of obtaining correct address.

Should subscriptions be forwarded in aggregate, the officer so forwarding will please enclose the names of the several subscribers. Subscriptions may be remitted to the Treasurer,

Prof. A. E. CHURCH, West Point, N. Y.

Signed, etc., by Executive Committee.

On motion, it was declared the purpose of the Committee to include the cases of such officers as may die after the war from wounds received as before mentioned, and that in addition to the name, etc., and rank in the Regular Army, should be recorded also the rank, in Volunteers, of officers named.

On motion, the Finance Committee were instructed to inquire the amount which might probably be raised by proposed plan of subscription; and the same Committee was authorized to direct such incidental expenditures as are from time to time required.

W. A. ELDERKIN,
First Lieut. 1st Artillery, U. S. Army,
President.

First Lieut. C. C. PARSONS, 4th Artillery, U. S. Army,
Secretary.

* * * * *

West Point, N. Y., Nov. 24, 1863.

The Executive Committee met upon call of the Secretary, pursuant to terms of last adjournment. Prof. Church in the chair. Present—all the members except Col. Bowman and Capt. Benet.

The minutes of the last meeting were read and accepted. The Secretary stated that he had called the meeting in order to answer inquiries in regard to action taken since the last adjournment. The minutes of the meeting and the Circular afterwards adopted had been placed by the President of the Committee in the hands of Brig.-General Totten, Chief Engineer and Inspector of the Academy. No response had been returned thereto.

Whereupon, after full discussion, the following resolutions were adopted:

The purpose and plan of action of this Organization having been laid before the Chief Engineer and Inspector of the Academy and no objection having been returned, it is

Resolved, 1st. That the Secretary, under supervision of the Finance Committee, be directed to procure the printing of (blank to be filled by the Secretary) copies of the Circular, to be distributed as contemplated, and also the publication of the same in the most suitable journals.

2d. That application in the name of the Executive Committee be made to the Secretary of War for permission to erect the *Battle Monument* at this post.

3d. That the subscriptions necessary to defray the expenses to be incurred by the First Resolution be at once solicited, such subscriptions to be regarded as part of the permanent fund.

4th. That the Secretary be permitted to sign the name of each member of the Executive Committee to the above Circular, and all corresponding papers properly authorized.

5th. That the Finance Committee be directed to procure a book in which shall be permanently recorded the names of all subscribers to the funds of the Association.

6th. That copies of the proceedings, resolutions, etc., most prominently setting forth the plans and purposes of the organization be forwarded by the Secretary to officers of the Regular Army high in command, with the request that they furnish responses which shall be appended to the Circular for general distribution.

The Secretary was directed to add to the Circular so much as is necessary to carry out the intention of the 6th Resolution.

* * * * * *

West Point, N. Y., Dec. 15, 1863.

The Secretary reported that, conformably with a Resolution of the last meeting, he had ordered the printing of fifty copies each of Submitted Circulars and Extracts from Minutes, and asked further instructions.

A list of names including sixteen was determined upon by the Committee, to whom these papers should be forwarded and their responses appended to the Circular.

The Committee on Finance, through the Chairman, reported that from calculation upon the present basis of subscription, the amount to be realized would approximate to $20,000. The Committee on Site were directed to report as early as convenient.

* * * * * *

West Point, N. Y., Jan. 28, 1864.

The Secretary presented as subject for action printed Circulars, of which 2600 copies had been ordered, embodying, in addition to the first Circular of the Committee, extracts from all the responses thus far received — namely, from Maj.-Genls. McClellan, Wool, Grant, Thomas, Buell, Hooker and Meade, and Brig.-Gen. Meigs, Q.-M.-General of the Army; also a plan for the Monument from Genl. Meigs. The Chairman stated that he had received a letter from Gen. Gibbon containing certain suggestions laid before the Committee. On motion and after discussion upon the ways and means of issuing these, the Circular was adopted.

* * * * * *

West Point, N. Y., Feby. 5, 1864.

The Secretary submitted a letter from Major R. Williams, A. A. G., suggesting the printing of about 3000 Circulars, to be forwarded to him, upon which he would forward them to every officer of the Regular Army.

Upon motion, it was directed that the Circulars of the first edition be so changed as to include in the object of the Monument a Memorial to the Enlisted Men who shall fall, etc., and that in the pro rata subscription $1.00 be added for Enlisted Men.

* * * * * *

West Point, N. Y., Feby. 24, 1864.

The Secretary announced as business before the Committee that a vacancy had been created by reason of Capt. Benet having been ordered from the post.

On motion, Capt. T. J. Treadwell, Ordnance Corps, was elected to fill the vacancy.

The letter of Maj. F. M. Etting, Additional Paymaster, enquiring in regard to those included within the appeal and objects of the Executive Committee, being submitted, the Secretary was directed to reply that the term "Regular Officer" was supposed to include those enumerated on page 110 (marked A), Army Register, dated Washington, April 1, 1863.

* * * * * *

West Point, N. Y., April 19, 1864.

The following resolutions, providing for the inaugurating of the Monument, were unanimously passed :

1st. *Resolved:* That the ceremony of inauguration of the BATTLE MONUMENT take place the 15th of June, next.

2d. That the Committees on Site and Design be directed to so determine that a position for the Monument shall be selected and reported to the Executive Committee at its next meeting.

3d. That the Committee on Ceremonies be directed to prepare and report at the next meeting a programme of exercises for the day of inauguration.

4th. That Maj.-General McClellan be invited in the name of the Executive Committee to deliver the Inaugural Address.

Upon further motion, it was directed that the Chairman appoint three other members of the Executive Committee to confer with the Committee on Ceremonies upon the drawing up of the Programme in accordance with the 3d Resolution; whereupon the chairman appointed Maj. Chambliss, Captains McAlister and Treadwell as such additional members. Upon further motion, the Secretary was directed to tender the thanks of the Executive Committee, and thus of the Army, to

Major R. Williams, Asst. Adjt.-General, for the especial service he has rendered to this project by procuring the directing, franking and forwarding of 2500 copies of the Committee's last circular to all officers of the army.

On May 3, 1864, as a result of the foregoing, the Secretary laid before the Committee a letter from Maj.-General McClellan, accepting the Committee's invitation to deliver the Inaugural Address upon the 15th of June, next, whereupon it was directed that the correspondence upon this invitation be entered in the minutes of the evening.

This correspondence was not so entered, and no trace of it can be found.

The dedication of Trophy Point as the site of the Monument took place in accordance with the foregoing resolutions.

Its interest was heightened by the presence of the shattered but still steady remnants of the 3d, 6th, 7th, and 12th Regiments, U. S. Infantry, the bands of these and of the 5th Artillery, and the permanent party of Fort Columbus, N. Y. Harbor, preceded in procession by the U. S. Corps of Cadets and the Military Academy Band.

It was also distinguished throughout by that deep solemnity of feeling which was eminently due to the occasion.

Brig.-General Anderson officiated as chief marshal, and Rev. Drs. French and Sprole as chaplains.

DEDICATION OF SITE
ON
TROPHY POINT

DEDICATION OF SITE ON TROPHY POINT, ON JUNE 15, 1864

West Point, June 15, 1864.

PROGRAMME OF CEREMONIES.

PROCESSION.

Assistant Marshal, Capt. Wilkins, 3d Infantry.
   I. Military Academy Band.
   II. Battalion of Cadets.

Assistant Marshal, Capt. Smith, 8th Infantry.
   III. Detachments of troops stationed at and visiting the post.
   IV. Carriage containing the President of the Executive Committee, the Chief Marshal, and State Executives.

Assistant Marshal, Lieut. Hamilton, 2d Artillery.
  V. Senior member of the Committee, Orator, and Chaplains.
  VI. The Executive Committee.
  VII. Military and Academic Staff, Board of Visitors, and Invited Guests.

Assistant Marshals, { Capt. Davies, 16th Infantry.
                      { Capt. Barlow, Engineers.

PROCEEDINGS.

   I. Prayer . . . . Rev. Dr. French
  II. Music . . . . Military Academy Band
              "Hail Columbia."
 III. Oration . . . . Maj.-General McClellan
 IV. Music . . . . Military Academy Band
   "Star Spangled Banner" and "Yankee Doodle."
  V. Benediction . . . . . Rev. Dr. Sprole
 VI. Dirge . . . . Military Academy Band

PRAYERS.

I.

For the Country.

Almighty God, fountain of order, source of all law in heaven and in earth, who hast ordained that men shall exist in organized communities, who, in the days of our fathers, didst bring forth, in the hour of darkness, the starry order of American institutions, for which we praise and bless Thee, we commend our country, now and ever, with all its interests, to Thy protecting care. May Thy fatherly hand ever be extended for perpetual benedictions over this land, kept by Thee through ages for us; over its people, trained by Thee so long for a sublime heaven; its Constitution, fruit of Thy teachings in history; its Union, blending human diversities into one chorus acceptable to Thee, the lover of concord; and its laws, uniting, after the model of Thine, mercy with justice, and liberty with order. From Thine own deeps of purity and love, breathe into the whole American people, by Thy spirit, and through all-subduing charity, that sacred affection, love to our country. Remove for ever from them, the spirit of sedition, conspiracy, rebellion, and give them steadfast loyalty, and unswerving allegiance. Specially do we implore Thee thus to turn the hearts of those who are now in arms against authority. In the contest to which we have been summoned for defending the precious trusts handed on from our fathers, wilt Thou send us now prosperity, and grant us victory. O, let not the impassioned yearnings of a great people for unity, for nationality, for beneficent order, for a lasting tranquillity, be in vain. May their lavish sacrifices, their patriotic efforts, their patient endurances, their silent tears falling in so many saddened homesteads, not be fruitless, but be regarded by Thee, through Thy Son, for benedictions, and by distant posterities, blessed through them, for abundant honor. So may we be through coming time, one people, fearing Thee and working righteousness, glorifying Thy name, and elevating Thy whole human family. All of which we ask through Jesus Christ our Saviour. Amen.

II.

For the President of the United States, and all others in Authority.

O everlasting God, by whose eternal providence all things and all men have their stations and their works, wherein they may serve Thee, and do good to Thy creatures, we ask for Thy blessing on the President of the United States, and all others in authority. Called by Thee to great duties, may they find in Thee strength and wisdom for all. Bestow upon them all good gifts for government; inspire them with wisest counsels and heroic resolutions. Console them in their difficult tasks with the consciousness of duty done, of intentions sincerely placed on the public welfare, justice, and honor; of the sympathy of upright men; of the appreciation of other ages; and of Thine own merciful and forgiving approval. In this life may Thy providence guard them. In mortal senses may Thy spirit so guide them, that they may hereafter serve and glorify Thee in a better country that is an heavenly; through Him who taught the rules and procured the spirit for all human duties, our teacher, our model, our restorer, Jesus Christ our Lord. Amen.

III.

For the Army and Navy and their Schools.

Lord God of Hosts, who hast determined the union of power with law throughout all Thy works, and for all communities of men, be pleased to receive into Thy almighty and most gracious protection the Army and Navy of the United States. Fill the whole public force with the spirit of patriotism and self-sacrifice, with an inspiring conviction of the glory of the cause for which it is now called to dare and to endure. May its persons be defended by Thee in danger and encouraged to all deeds of heroism by the affection and honor of a grateful country. And may both its schools be the nurseries of pure, accomplished, and brave men, and be continually sending forth on land and sea those who may render, in peace and war, good and faithful service to the public. So may the people of our land, under the shelter of good laws, in peace and quietness, serve Thee our God, and lead lives of all godliness and honesty, to the glory of Thy name, and the promotion of human welfare, through Him who gave the example of self-sacrifice, dying for us that we might live with Thee, Thy Son, our Saviour. Amen.

For a Blessing on the Occasion.

O God of the spirits of all flesh, calling the generations from the beginning, and, since the first transgression, bidding dust return to dust again, may this spot, consecrated now to the memory of heroes, be hallowed also to the benefit of the living. May those brought here for their last repose be the temples of Thy Holy Spirit, and leave spotless records of lives made glorious by duty conscientiously done, so that the wayfarer, lingering and musing here, may find his soul enkindled to ennobling emulations. And may this whole assembly look this day from the grave to the life immortal. Here, in a temple not made with hands, where the mountains rise, the river flows, the valley slumbers, all telling of Thee and of Thy unspeakable perfection, may thoughts arise within us answering to the majesty of Thy glorious works. Here may we consecrate ourselves anew to the love of Thee, the love of man, the love of Thy will; to the doing of justice, to the loving of mercy, and to walking humbly with Thee our God: that so, when we too shall lie down in the dust, we may be Thy children, justified, sanctified, and prepared to be glorified, all through Him who has opened the way to Thee, and who, to inbreathe these great affections, has taught us when we pray to say:

Our Father, who art in heaven, Hallowed be Thy name. Thy Kingdom come. Thy will be done on earth, as it is in heaven. Give us this day our daily bread. And forgive us our trespasses, as we forgive those who trespass against us. And lead us not into temptation: But deliver us from evil. For Thine is the kingdom and the power and the glory, for ever and ever. Amen.

After the prayer, Prof. French said:

I am requested, on behalf of the officers of the army, and of the local authorities and residents, to express their sentiments and wishes, and most earnestly to ask that these may be respected. To all of us, the day is a solemn one; to military feelings, ever confronted with death, the occasion is the same as though cherished comrades were now to be laid in the grave. They ask, therefore, that this hour and this day may be invested with the decorum attached to funeral solemnities, that no demonstration of any kind be made on the ground or afterward, but that all may enter into the spirit and motive of the solemn occasion which calls us here in reverence, before Almighty God, to set apart a portion of his foot-stool for the remains of those who shall fall in this war in the defense of the Constitution, the Union, the welfare, and the national honor of the United States.

General Anderson's introduction of the orator:

Fellow-citizens, members of the corps of cadets, and brother soldiers, I have the pleasure of going through the form of introducing to you one who is better known to you than I who introduce him,— the orator of the day, Major-General George B. McClellan.

ORATION BY
GENERAL GEORGE B. McCLELLAN

ALL nations have days sacred to the remembrance of joy and of grief. They have thanksgivings for success, fasting and prayers in the hour of humiliation and defeat, triumphs and pæans to greet the living and laurel-crowned victor. They have obsequies and eulogies for the warrior slain on the field of battle. Such is the duty we are to perform to-day. The poetry, the histories, the orations of antiquity, all resound with the clang of arms; they dwell rather upon rough deeds of war, than the gentle arts of peace. They have preserved to us the names of heroes, and the memory of their deeds, even to this distant day. Our own Old Testament teems with the narrations of the brave actions and heroic deaths of Jewish patriots, while the New Testament of our meek and suffering Saviour often selects the soldier and his weapons to typify and illustrate religious heroism and duty. These stories of the actions of the dead have frequently survived, in the lapse of ages, the names of those whose fall was thus commemorated centuries ago. But, although we know not now the names of all the brave men who fought and fell upon the plain of Marathon, in the pass of

Thermopylæ, and on the hills of Palestine, we have not lost the memory of their examples. As long as the warm blood courses the veins of man, as long as the human heart beats high and quick at the recital of brave deeds and patriotic sacrifices, so long will the lesson still incite generous men to emulate the heroism of the past.

Among the Greeks, it was the custom that the fathers of the most valiant of the slain should pronounce the eulogies of the dead. Sometimes it devolved upon their great statesmen and orators to perform this mournful duty. Would that a new Demosthenes, or a second Pericles, could arise and take my place to-day, for he would find a theme worthy of his most brilliant powers, of his most touching eloquence. I stand here now, not as an orator, but as a whilom commander, and in the place of the fathers of the most valiant dead; as their comrade, too, on many a hard-fought field, against domestic and foreign foe — in early youth and mature manhood — moved by all the love that David felt when he poured forth his lamentations for the mighty father and son who fell on Mount Gilboa. God knows that David's love for Jonathan was no more deep than mine for the tried friends of many long and eventful years, whose names are to be recorded upon the structure that is to rise upon this spot. Would that his more than mortal eloquence could grace my lips and do justice to the theme!

We have met to-day, my comrades, to do honor to our own dead; brothers united to us by the closest and dearest ties, who have freely given their lives for their country in this war — so just and righteous so long as its purpose is to crush rebellion, and to save our nation from the infinite evils of dismemberment. Such an occasion as this should call forth the deepest and noblest emotions of our nature — pride, sorrow, and prayer: pride that our country has possessed such sons; sorrow that she has lost them; prayer that she may have others like them; that we and our successors may adorn her annals as they have done, and that when our parting hour arrives, whenever and however it may be, our souls may be prepared for the great change.

We have assembled to consecrate a cenotaph which shall remind our children's children, in the distant future, of their fathers' struggles in the days of the great rebellion. This monument is to perpetuate the memory of a portion only of those who have fallen for the nation in this unhappy war — it is dedicated to the officers and soldiers of the regular army. Yet this is done in no class or exclusive spirit, and in the act we remember, with reverence and love, our comrades of the volunteers who have so gloriously fought and fallen by our side. Each State will, no doubt, commemorate in some fitting way the services of its sons who abandoned the avocations of peace and shed their blood in the ranks of the volunteers. How richly they have earned a nation's love, a nation's gratitude, with what heroism they have confronted death, have wrested victory from a stubborn foe, and have illustrated defeat, it well becomes me to say, for it has been my lot to command them on many a sanguinary field. I know that I but echo the feeling of the regulars when I award the high credit they deserve to their brave brethren of the volunteers.

But we of the regular army have no States to look to for the honors due our dead. We belong to the whole country, and can neither expect nor desire the general government to make a perhaps invidious distinction in our favor. We are few in number, a small band of comrades, united by peculiar and very binding ties; for with many of us our friendships were commenced in boyhood, when we rested here in the shadow of the granite hills which look down upon us where we stand; with others the ties of brotherhood were formed in more mature years, while fighting among the rugged mountains and the fertile valleys of Mexico — within hearing of the eternal waves of the Pacific, or in the lonely grandeur of the great plains of the far West. With all, our love and confidence have been cemented by common dangers and sufferings, on the toilsome march, in the dreary bivouac, and amid the clash of arms, and in the presence of death on scores of battle-fields. West Point, with her large heart, adopts us all—graduates and those appointed from civil life, officers and privates. In her eyes we are all her children, jealous of her fame, and eager to sustain her world-wide reputation. Generals and private soldiers, men who have cheerfully offered our all for our dear country, we stand here before this shrine, ever hereafter sacred to our dead, equals and brothers in the presence of the common death which awaits us all, perhaps on the same field and at the same hour. Such are the ties which unite us, the most endearing which exist among men; such the relations which bind us together, the closest of the sacred brotherhood of arms.

It has therefore seemed, and it is fitting, that we should erect upon this spot, so sacred to us all, an enduring monument to our dear brothers who have preceded us upon the path of peril and of honor, which it is the destiny of many of us to tread.

What is this regular army to which we belong?

Who were the men whose death merits such honors from the living?

What is the cause for which they have laid down their lives?

Our regular or permanent army is the nucleus which, in time of peace, preserves the military traditions of the nation, as well as the organization, science and instruction indispensable to modern armies. It may be regarded as co-eval with the nation. It derives its origin from the old Continental and State lines of the Revolution, whence, with some interruptions and many changes, it has attained its present condition. In fact, we may with propriety go even beyond the Revolution to seek the roots of our genealogical tree in the old French wars, for the Cis-Atlantic campaigns of the Seven Years' War were not confined to the "red men scalping each other by the great lakes of North America," and it was in them that our ancestors first participated as Americans in the large operations of civilized armies. American regiments then fought on the banks of the St. Lawrence and the Ohio, on the shores of Ontario and Lake George, on the islands of the Caribbean and in South America. Louisburg, Quebec, Duquesne, the Moro, and Porto Bello, attest the value of the provincial troops, and in that school were educated such soldiers as Washington, Putnam, Lee, Montgomery and Gates. These, and men like Greene, Knox, Wayne and Steuben, were the fathers of our permanent army, and under them our troops acquired that discipline and steadiness which enabled them to meet upon equal terms, and often to defeat, the tried veterans of England. The study of the history of the Revolution, and a perusal of the despatches of Washington, will convince the most skeptical of the value of the permanent army in achieving our independence and establishing the civil edifice which we are now fighting to preserve.

The War of 1812 found the army on a footing far from adequate to the emergency, but it was rapidly increased, and of the new generation of soldiers many proved equal to the requirements of the occasion. Lundy's Lane, Chippewa, Queenstown, Plattsburg, New Orleans — all bear witness to the gallantry of the regulars.

Then came an interval of more than thirty years of external peace, marked by so many changes in the organization and strength of the regular army, and broken at times by tedious and bloody Indian wars. Of these the most remarkable were the Black Hawk War, in which our troops met unflinchingly a foe as relentless, and far more destructive than the Indians — that terrible scourge, the cholera; and the tedious Florida War, where, for many years, the Seminoles eluded in the pestilential swamps our utmost efforts, and in which were displayed such traits of heroism as that commemorated by yonder monument to Dade and his command, "when all fell, save three, without an attempt to retreat." At last came the Mexican War, to replace Indian combats and the monotony of the frontier service, and for the first time in many years the mass of the regular army was concentrated, and took the principal part in the battles of that remarkable and romantic war. Palo Alto, Resaca, and Fort Brown, were the achievements of the regulars unaided; and as to the battles of Monterey, Buena Vista, Vera Cruz, Cerro Gordo, and the final triumphs in the valley, none can truly say that they could have been won without the regulars. When peace crowned our victories in the capital of the Montezumas, the army was at once dispersed over the long frontier, and engaged in harassing and dangerous wars with the Indians of the plains. Thus thirteen long years were spent, until the present war broke out, and the mass of the army was drawn in to be employed against a domestic foe.

I cannot proceed to the events of the recent past and the present without adverting to the gallant men who were so long of our number, but who have now gone to their last home; for no small portion of the glory of which we boast was reflected from such men as Taylor, Worth, Brady, Brooks, Totten, and Duncan.

There is a sad story of Venetian history that has moved many a heart, and often employed the poet's pen and the painter's pencil. It is of an old man whose long life was gloriously spent in the service of the state as a warrior and a statesman, and who, when his hair was white and his feeble limbs could scarce carry his bent form toward the grave, attained the highest honors that a Venetian citizen could reach. He was Doge of Venice. Convicted of treason against the state, he not only lost his life, but suffered beside a penalty which will endure as long as the name of Venice is remembered. The spot where his portrait should have hung in the great hall of the doge's palace was veiled with black, and there still remains the frame, with its black mass of canvas — and this vacant frame is the most conspicuous in the long line of effigies of illustrious doges!

Oh! that such a pall as that which replaces the portrait of Marino Faliero could conceal from history the names of those, once our comrades, who are now in arms against the flag under which we fought side by side in years gone by. But no veil can cover the anguish that fills our hearts when we look back upon the sad memory of the past, and recall the affection and respect we entertained toward men against whom it is our duty to act in mortal combat. Would that the courage, ability and steadfastness they displayed had been employed in the defense of the "Stars and Stripes" against a foreign foe, rather than in this gratuitous and unjustifiable rebellion, which could not be so long maintained but for the skill and energy of those, our former comrades!

But we have reason to rejoice that upon this day, so sacred and so eventful for us, one grand old mortal monument of the past still lifts high his head amongst us, and graces by his presence the consecration of this tomb of his children. We may well be proud that we have been commanded by the hero who purchased victory with his blood near the great waters of Niagara, who repeated and eclipsed the achievements of Cortez; who, although a consummate and confident commander, ever preferred, when duty and honor would permit, the olive branch of peace to the blood-stained laurels of war, and who stands, at the close of a long, glorious and eventful life, a living column of granite against which have beaten in vain alike the blandishments and the storms of treason. His name will ever be one of our proudest boasts and most moving inspirations. In long-distant ages, when this incipient monument has become venerable, moss-clad, and perhaps ruinous, when the names inscribed upon it shall seem, to those who pause to read them, indistinct mementos of an almost mythical past, the name of Winfield Scott will still be clear cut upon the memory of them all, like the still fresh carving upon the monuments of long-forgotten Pharaohs.

But it is time to approach the present.

In the war which now shakes the land to its foundation, the regular army has borne a most honorable part. Too few in numbers to act by themselves, regular regiments have participated in every great battle in the East, and in most of those west of the Alleghanies. Their terrible losses and diminished numbers prove that they have been in the thickest of the fights, and the testimony of their comrades and commanders shows with what undaunted heroism they have upheld their ancient renown. Their vigorous charges have often won the day, and in defeat they have more than once saved the army from destruction or terrible losses by the obstinacy with which they resisted overpowering numbers. They can refer with pride to the part they played upon the glorious fields of Mexico, and exult at the recollection of what they did at Manassas, Gaines's Mill, Malvern, Antietam, Shiloh, Stone River, Gettysburg, and the great battles just fought from the Rapidan to the Chickahominy. They can also point to the officers who have risen among them and achieved great deeds for their country in this war; — to the living warriors whose names are on the nation's tongue and heart, too numerous to be repeated here, yet not one of whom I could willingly omit.

But perhaps the proudest episode in the history of the regular army is that touching instance of fidelity on the part of the non-commissioned officers and privates who, treacherously made prisoners in Texas, resisted every temptation to violate their oath and desert their flag. Offered commissions in the rebel service, money and land freely tendered them, they all scorned the inducements held out to them, submitted to every hardship, and when at last exchanged, avenged themselves on the field of battle for the unavailing insult offered their integrity. History affords no brighter example of honor than that of these brave men, tempted, as I blush to say they were, by some of their former officers, who, having themselves proved false to their flag, endeavored to seduce the men who had often followed them in combat, and who had naturally regarded them with respect and love.

Such is the regular army — such its history and antecedents — such its officers and men. It needs no herald to trumpet forth its praises; it can proudly appeal to the numerous fields, from the tropics to the frozen banks of the St. Lawrence, from the Atlantic to the Pacific, fertilized by the blood and whitened by the bones of its members. But I will not pause to eulogize it. Let its deeds speak for it; they are more eloquent than tongue of mine.

Why are we here to-day?

This is not the funeral of one brave warrior, nor even of the harvest of death on a single battle-field, but these are the obsequies of the best and bravest of the children of the land, who have fallen in actions almost numberless, many of them among the most sanguinary and desperate of which history bears record. The men whose names and deeds we now seek to perpetuate, rendering them the highest honor in our power, have fallen wherever armed rebellion showed its front — in far-distant New Mexico, in the broad valley of the Mississippi, on the bloody hunting-grounds of Kentucky, in the mountains of Tennessee, amid the swamps of Carolina, on the fertile fields of Maryland, and in the blood-stained thickets of Virginia. They were of all the grades — from the general officer to the private; of all ages — from the gray-haired veteran, of fifty years' service, to the beardless youth; of all degrees of cultivation — from the man of science to the uneducated boy. It is not necessary, nor is it possible, to repeat the mournful yet illustrious roll of dead heroes whom we have met to honor. Nor shall I attempt to name all of those who most merit praise — simply a few who will exemplify the classes to which they belong.

Among the last slain, but among the first in honor and reputation, was that hero of twenty battles — John Sedgwick. Gentle and kind as a woman, brave as a brave man can be, honest, sincere, and able — he was a model that all may strive to imitate, but whom few can equal. In the terrible battles which just preceded his death, he had occasion to display the highest qualities of a commander and a soldier; yet after escaping the stroke of death when men fell around him by thousands, he at last met his fate at a moment of comparative quiet, by the ball of a single rifleman. He died as a soldier would choose to die — with truth in his heart, and a sweet, tranquil smile upon his face. Alas! our great nation possesses few sons like true John Sedgwick.

Like him fell, too, at the very head of their corps, the white-haired Mansfield, after a long career of usefulness, illustrated by his skill and cool courage at Fort Brown, Monterey, and Buena Vista; John F. Reynolds and Reno, both in the full vigor of manhood and intellect — men who had proved their ability and chivalry on many a field in Mexico and in this civil war, gallant gentlemen of whom their country had much to hope, had it pleased God to spare their lives. Lyon fell in the prime of life, leading his little army against superior numbers, his brief career affording a brilliant example of patriotism and ability. The impetuous Kearny, and such brave generals as Richardson, Williams, Terrill, Stevens, Weed, Strong, Saunders and Hayes, lost their lives while in the midst of a career of usefulness. Young Bayard, so like the most renowned of his name, that "knight above fear and above reproach," was cut off too early for his country, and that excellent staff-officer, Colonel Garesché, fell while gallantly doing his duty.

No regiments can spare such gallant, devoted and able commanders as Rossell, Davis, Gore, Simmons, Bailey, Putnam and Kingsbury — all of whom fell in the thickest of the combat — some of them veterans, and others young in service, all good men and well-beloved.

Our batteries have partially paid their terrible debt to fate in the loss of such commanders as Greble, the first to fall in this war, Benson, Hazzard, Smead, De Hart, Hazlitt, and those gallant boys, Kirby, Woodruff, Dimmick and Cushing; while the engineers lament the promising and gallant Wagner and Cross.

Beneath remote battle-fields rest the corpses of the heroic McRea, Reed, Bascom, Stone, Sweet, and many other company officers.

Besides these were hosts of veteran sergeants, corporals and privates who had fought under Scott in Mexico, or contended in many combats with the savages of the far West and Florida; and, mingled with them, young soldiers who, courageous, steady and true, met death unflinchingly, without the hope of personal glory. These men, in their more humble sphere, served their country with as much faith and honor as the most illustrious generals, and all of them with perfect singleness of heart. Although their names may not live in history, their actions, loyalty, and courage will live. Their memories will long be preserved in their regiments, for there were many of them who merited as proud a distinction as that accorded to the "first grenadier of France," or to that other Russian soldier who gave his life for his comrades.

But there is another class of men who have gone from us since this war commenced, whose fate it was not to die in battle, but who are none the less entitled to be mentioned here. There was Sumner, a brave, honest, chivalrous veteran, of more than half a century's service, who had confronted death unflinchingly on scores of battlefields, had shown his gray head serene and cheerful where death most revelled, who more than once told me that he believed and hoped that his long career would end amid the din of battle — he died at home from the effects of the hardships of his campaigns.

The most excellent soldier, the elegant C. F. Smith, whom many of us remember to have seen so often on this plain, with his superb bearing, escaped the bullet to fall a victim to the disease which has deprived the army of so many of its best soldiers.

John Buford, cool and intrepid; Mitchell, eminent in science; Plummer, Palmer, and many other officers and men, lost their lives by sickness contracted in the field.

But I cannot close this long list of glorious martyrs without paying a sacred debt of official duty and personal friendship. There was one dead soldier who possessed peculiar claims upon my love and gratitude. He was an ardent patriot, an unselfish man, a true soldier, the beau ideal of a staff-officer — he was my aide-de-camp, Colonel Colburn.

There is a lesson to be drawn from the death and services of these glorious men which we should read for the present and future benefit of the nation. War in these modern days is a science, and it should now be clear to the most prejudiced that for the organization and command of armies, and the high combinations of strategy, perfect familiarity with the theoretical science of war is requisite. To count upon success when the plans or execution of campaigns are intrusted to men who have no knowledge of war, is as idle as to expect the legal wisdom of a Story or a Kent from a skilful physician.

But what is the honorable and holy cause for which these men laid down their lives, and for which the nation still demands the sacrifice of the precious blood of so many of her children?

Soon after the close of the Revolutionary War, it was found that the Confederacy, which had grown up during that memorable contest, was fast falling to pieces from its own weight. The central power was too weak; it could only recommend to the different States such measures as seemed best; and it possessed no real power to legislate, because it lacked the executive force to compel obedience to its laws. The national credit and self-respect had disappeared, and it was feared by the friends of human liberty throughout the world that ours was but another added to the long list of fruitless attempts at self-government. The nation was evidently upon the brink of ruin and dissolution, when, some eighty years ago, many of the wisest and most patriotic of the land met to seek a remedy for the great evils which threatened to destroy the great work of the Revolution. Their sessions were long, and often stormy; for a time the most sanguine doubted the possibility of a successful termination to their labors. But, from amidst the conflict of sectional interests, of party prejudices, and of personal selfishness, the spirit of wisdom and conciliation at length evoked the Constitution, under which we have lived so long.

It was not formed in a day, but was the result of patient labor, of lofty wisdom, and of the purest patriotism. It was at last adopted by the people of all the States — although by some reluctantly — not as being exactly what all desired, but as being the best possible under the circumstances. It was accepted as giving us a form of government under which the nation might live happily and prosper, so long as the people should continue to be influenced by the same sentiments which actuated those who formed it, and which would not be liable to destruction from internal causes, so long as the people preserved the recollection of the miseries and calamities which led to its adoption.

Under this beneficent Constitution the progress of the nation was unexampled in history. The rights and liberties of its citizens were secure at home and abroad; vast territories were rescued from the control of the savage and the wild beast, and added to the domain of civilization and the Union.

The arts, the sciences, and commerce, grew apace; our flag floated upon every sea, and we took our place among the great nations of the earth.

But under the smooth surface of prosperity upon which we glided swiftly, with all sails set before the summer breeze, dangerous reefs were hidden which now and then caused ripples upon the surface, and made anxious the more cautious pilots. Elated by success, the ship swept on, the crew not heeding the warnings they received, forgetful of the dangers they escaped in the beginning of the voyage, and blind to the hideous maelstrom which gaped to receive and destroy them. The same elements of discordant sectional prejudices, interests, and institutions, which had rendered the formation of the Constitution so difficult, threatened more than once to destroy it. But for a long time the nation was so fortunate as to possess a series of political leaders who, to the highest abilities, united the same spirit of conciliation which animated the founders of the Republic, and thus for many years the threatened evils were averted. Time and long-continued good fortune obliterated the recollection of the calamities and wretchedness of the years preceding the adoption of the Constitution. Men forgot that conciliation, common interest, and mutual charity, had been the foundation and must be the support of our government — as is indeed the case with all governments and all the relations of life. At length men appeared with whom sectional and personal prejudices and interests outweighed all considerations for the general good. Extremists of one section furnished the occasion, eagerly seized as a pretext by equally extreme men in the other, for abandoning the pacific remedies and protection afforded by the Constitution, and seeking redress for possible future evils in war and the destruction of the Union.

Stripped of all sophistry and side issues, the direct cause of the war as it presented itself to the honest and patriotic citizens of the North, was simply this: Certain States, or rather, a portion of the inhabitants of certain States, feared, or professed to fear, that injury would result to their rights and property from the elevation of a particular party to power. Although the Constitution and the actual condition of the government provided them with a peaceable and sure protection against the apprehended evil, they preferred to seek security in the destruction of the government, which could protect them, and in the use of force against the national troops holding a national fortress.

To efface the insult offered our flag; to save ourselves from the fate of the divided republics of Italy and South America, to preserve our government from destruction, to enforce its just power and laws, to maintain our very existence as a nation — these were the causes that compelled us to draw the sword.

Rebellion against a government like ours, which contains the means of self-adjustment, and a pacific remedy for evils, should never be confounded with a revolution against despotic power, which refuses redress of wrongs. Such a rebellion cannot be justified upon ethical grounds, and the only alternative for our choice is its suppression, or the destruction of our nationality. At such a time as this, and in such a struggle, political partisanship should be merged in a true and brave patriotism, which thinks only of the good of the whole country.

It was in this cause, and with these motives, that so many of our comrades gave their lives, and to this we are all personally pledged in all honor and fidelity. Shall such a devotion as that of our dead comrades be of no avail? Shall it be said in after ages that we lacked the vigor to complete the work thus begun? that, after all these noble lives freely given, we hesitated, and failed to keep straight on until our land was saved? Forbid it, Heaven, and give us firmer, truer hearts than that!

Oh, spirits of the valiant dead, souls of our slain heroes, lend us your own indomitable will, and if it be permitted you to commune with those still chained by the trammels of mortality, hover around us in the midst of danger and tribulation, cheer the firm, strengthen the weak, that none may doubt the salvation of the republic and the triumph of our grand old flag!

In the midst of the storms which toss our ship of state, there is one great beacon light, to which we can ever turn with confidence and hope. It cannot be that this great nation has played its part in history; it cannot be that our sun, which arose with such bright promises for the future, has already set for ever. It must be the intention of the overruling Deity that this land, so long the asylum of the oppressed, the refuge of civil and religious liberty, shall again stand forth in bright relief, united, purified, and chastened by our trials, as an example and encouragement for those who desire the progress of the human race. It is not given to our weak intellects to understand the steps of Providence as they occur; we comprehend them only as we look upon them in the far distant past.

So is it now.

We cannot unravel the seemingly tangled skein of the purposes of the Creator — they are too high and far-reaching for our limited minds. But all history and his own revealed word teach us that his ways, although inscrutable, are ever righteous. Let us then honestly and manfully play our part, seek to understand and perform our whole duty, and trust unwaveringly in the beneficence of the God who led our ancestors across the sea, and sustained them afterward, amid dangers more appalling even than those encountered by his own chosen people in their great exodus. He did not bring us here in vain, nor has he supported us thus far for naught. If we do our duty and trust in him, he will not desert us in our need.

Firm in our faith that God will save our country, we now dedicate this site to the memory of brave men, to loyalty, patriotism, and honor.

BENEDICTION.

May the God of our fathers and our God, succeed with his divine benediction the solemn and interesting services of this occasion. May he conduct, by his gracious providence, the work commenced to-day to successful completion. May the monument here to be raised in honor of the illustrious dead, inspire with all the ardor of a sound Christian patriotism, the soldiers of our common country here trained for its defence; may it prove to them a constant remembrancer of their mortality, and keep alive upon the altar of their hearts the flame of devotion to God, to country, to the Union, the Constitution, and the immutable principles of truth and justice; and may the blessing of the triune God, the Father, Son, and Holy Spirit, be with you all. Amen.

West Point, N. Y., October 20, 1864.

On the call of the Secretary of the Association, First Lieutenant C. C. Parsons, 4th Artillery, a meeting of the officers of the Army, present at the Post, was held, for the transaction of such business in regard to the " Battle Monument " as might be brought before them. Prof. H. L. Kendrick in the chair.

The Secretary having been ordered from the Post, his resignation was tendered and accepted, and upon motion Captain F. L. Guenther, 5th Artillery, was elected to fill the vacancy thus occurring.

Upon motion, it was *Resolved*. That all officers of the Army, present at the Post, on duty or otherwise, be constituted a " Monument Committee." A motion that the Executive Committee of the Association should consist of the President, Treasurer and Secretary, and eight other members, was adopted.

Upon motion, the following officers were elected to constitute the Executive Committee, viz.:

Brig.-Gen. Geo. W. Cullum, *President*
Professor A. E. Church, *Treasurer*
Captain F. L. Guenther, 5th Artillery, *Secretary*
Colonel H. M. Black
Captain George H. Mendall, U. S. Engineers
Captain Lorenzo Lorain, 3d Artillery

Captain A. K. Arnold, 5th Cavalry
Captain A. T. Smith, 8th Infantry
Captain R. M. Hill, Ordnance Department
Lieut. H. B. Noble, 8th Infantry
Assistant Surgeon E. S. Dunster, Medical Dept.

Upon motion, it was

Resolved. That the thanks of the Association be tendered to the retiring Secretary, First Lieut. C. C. Parsons, 4th Artillery, for the zealous and able manner in which he has performed the duties of his office.

There being no further business before it, the meeting, upon motion, adjourned to meet again on the call of the Secretary.

F. L. Guenther, Captain 5th Artillery,
Secretary.

At some time not shown by the record an invitation to submit designs for the monument was issued by the Committee on Design. To what extent responses were obtained and what their character does not appear.

The invitation was as follows:

The BATTLE MONUMENT EXECUTIVE COMMITTEE will receive DESIGNS for the MONUMENT TO BE ERECTED AT WEST POINT, N. Y., to the Memory of the OFFICERS and ENLISTED MEN of the REGULAR ARMY who shall have fallen during the present war, as follows :

Sufficient expanse of surface is required to receive inscriptions of the name, rank, place of decease, etc., etc., of all

Officers of the Regular Army who shall have fallen during the war, and a general tablet for the enlisted men.

In connection with the monument, should be embraced a plan for a mausoleum, or place of interment, for the remains of such officers as may be brought to West Point for burial.

Full drawings, with the usual details, must be made, accompanied by an estimate of the cost — this not to exceed $25,000.

A premium of $250 will be paid for the design which is finally accepted.

It is desirable that designs be sent in as early as possible, in order that they may be carefully considered before a selection is made.

Further particulars may be obtained by addressing the Secretary at West Point, N. Y.

   A. H. Bowman, Col. of Engrs., *Chairman*,
   H. B. Clitz, Lieut.-Col. and Comdt.,
   W. A. Elderkin, First Lieut. 1st Art.,
         Committee on Design.
C. C. Parsons, First Lieut. 4th Art., *Secretary.*

* * * * * *

During the period from October, 1864, until the call of General Schofield of Sept. 9, 1878, the funds of the Association had been gradually accumulating under the admirable management of the Treasurer, Professor Church. Upon his death a meeting was called pursuant to the following circular:

U. S. Military Academy, West Point, N. Y.,
     September 9, 1878.

All officers of the army on duty at West Point are requested to attend a meeting at the Officers'

Mess at 7.30 this evening to transact important business appertaining to the *Battle Monument* Association.

A full attendance is respectfully desired.

J. M. Schofield,
Major-General and Superintendent.

This meeting of the officers of the Army on duty at West Point was held in the Officers' Mess at 7.30 P. M. Monday, the 9th of September, 1878, Major-General J. M. Schofield, Superintendent and ex-officio President of the Battle Monument Association, in the chair.

The President stated the object of the meeting to be to elect officers and fill vacancies upon the Executive Committee occasioned by death and by removal from the Post.

On motion the following officers were unanimously elected an Executive Committee in addition to

1st. Major-General J. M. Schofield, Superintendent, *President.*
2d. Lieut.-Colonel Thos. H. Neill, 6th Cavalry, Commandant of Cadets [*Ex-officio* members], viz:—
3d. Professor Peter S. Michie.
4th. Professor George L. Andrews (*Treasurer*).
5th. Professor Junius B. Wheeler.
6th. Professor Charles W. Larned.

7th. Professor Edgar W. Bass.
8th. Professor Guido N. Lieber.
9th. Surgeon Charles T. Alexander.
10th. First Lieut. Eric Burgland, Corps of Engineers.
11th. Captain William M. Wherry, 6th Infantry, *Secretary*.

On motion Professor George L. Andrews was unanimously elected Treasurer, and Colonel William M. Wherry, Secretary. On motion it was *Resolved*, That the Treasurer be directed to invest the funds of the association in U. S. registered bonds.

The Secretary was directed to furnish the "Army and Navy Journal" with a transcript of the record of these proceedings for publication.

On motion the meeting was adjourned.

J. M. Schofield, Major-General,
President.

Wm. M. Wherry, Bvt.-Colonel, U. S. A.,
Secretary.

* * * * * *

The first attempt to open the question of erection was made in the meeting of Oct. 22, 1885, called by General Merritt.

West Point, N. Y., Thursday, Oct. 22, 1885.

Proceedings of a meeting of the officers of the army stationed at West Point, N. Y., pursuant to a call of the Superintendent, Col. W. Merritt, 5th Regiment of Cavalry.

The meeting was called to order by Professor Michie.

On motion of Prof. Michie, Gen. Merritt was elected Chairman; Lieut. G. B. Davis was appointed Secretary by the Chair. At the request of the Chairman, Professor Geo. L. Andrews, the Treasurer of the Battle Monument Association, made an informal statement of the amount of the Monument fund. Lieut. W. C. Brown, Adjutant of the Military Academy, announced that he had in his possession the " Record of Proceedings of the Battle Monument Association." At the request of the Chairman, the record was produced by Lieut. Brown, and its contents were read by the Secretary.

The Chairman stated the purpose of the meeting to be to take some steps looking to the increase of the fund, and the erection of the Monument.

A motion that a committee of seven members be selected by the Chairman to investigate and report upon the question of erecting a monument was withdrawn.

A motion that the Executive Committee be directed to fill its vacancies, and report, was also withdrawn.

The Superintendent announced that he would call a meeting of the Executive Committee, at an early day, for the purpose of filling its vacancies and acting upon questions connected with the erection of the Monument.

On motion, the meeting then adjourned.

W. Merritt, Colonel 5th Cavalry,
Brevet Major-General, U. S. A.,
President.

Geo. B. Davis,
Secretary.

Nothing, however, was done towards actual realization of the project until the administration of Col. John M. Wilson as superintendent of the Academy. Deeming the time ripe for a movement in the matter, he addressed the following to the Treasurer of the Association:

Headquarters U. S. Military Academy,
West Point, N. Y., October 21, 1889.

General Geo. L. Andrews,
Treasurer Battle Monument Association.
Dear Sir:

Yours of the 21st instant, expressing a desire to resign the Treasurership of the Battle Monument Association is just received.

Will you please send me the list of subscribers to the Monument, if in your possession? If you have not the list, please inform me where it can be found.

I will at once enter into correspondence with such of the original subscribers as may be living and obtain their views as to what they would prefer in the shape of a Monument.

For myself, I think it might be well to use the fund either for the enlargement of the present Chapel, or the construction of a memorial hall in which would appear mural tablets giving the names of the officers who lost their lives in the defense of the Union.

As soon as I can get the views of those subscribers still living I will call a meeting of the officers here.

In the meantime may I ask you, for the present, to continue to hold the position of Treasurer which you have so acceptably filled for the past ten years?

    Yours very truly,

      JOHN M. WILSON, Colonel of Engineers,
        Superintendent.

The following is the letter of General Andrews referred to:

    U. S. Military Academy, West Point, N. Y.,
      Oct. 21, 1889.

Colonel John M. Wilson,
  Superintendent U. S. Military Academy,
    President of the Battle Monument Association.

Dear Sir:

Some time near the close of our Civil War, an association was formed at West Point for the purpose of having a monument erected here to the Officers of the Regular Army who fell in that war. The late Professor Church was elected Treasurer, and subscriptions were invited and received. The formation of the Association seems to have been somewhat loosely made; but on the decease of Professor Church in 1878, General Schofield, then Superintendent, as ex-officio President of the Association, called a meeting of the officers here stationed, who, it seems, constitute the Association. At that meeting I was elected Treasurer, and directed by vote of the members present to invest the funds and income of the Association in U. S.

Registered Bonds. Another meeting was called by General Merritt when Superintendent to consider what should be done in regard to the Monument, but no decisive action was taken.

The funds now in my hands as Treasurer are:

U. S. Currency 6 per cent. Bonds, par,	$3,000
U. S. 4 per cent. Registered Bonds, par,	47,300
Total,	$50,300

At the present market rate these Bonds would sell for about $63,500.

There were also donated by Act of Congress to Professor Church, Treasurer of the "Battle Monument Committee," fifty bronze cannon. These cannon were left stored at the New York Arsenal, Governor's Island, having been, as I understood, virtually delivered to Professor Church. However, more than a year ago, I was informed that unless the cannon were removed there was danger that they would be delivered to other parties. I wrote to General Benét, and learned from him that a new application for the cannon must be made, accompanied by evidence of authority for the new Treasurer to receive the same. I stated the case orally to General Parke, then Superintendent, but he was disinclined to do anything about the matter, and nothing further was done.

The foregoing statement is made agreeably to your oral request, and I would add that I wish to resign as soon as may be the position of Treasurer of the Association which I now hold. It is desirable that the new Treasurer be elected so that the transfer of bonds may be made before the books are closed for this quarter.

Respectfully yours,
GEO. L. ANDREWS,
Treasurer Battle Monument Association.

The following are the guns above described by Professor Andrews:

50	Cannon, Bronze, reserved at N. Y. Arsenal for Battle Monument.					
15	12-pounder	Field Guns, heavy,	. . .	U. S.	26,607
1	12	"	" "	. .	Rebel trophy,	1,375
16	24	"	" Howitzers	. .. .	U. S.	20,891
2	24	"	" "	.	Rebel trophies,	2,567
6	32	"	" . "	. . .	U. S.	11,457
5	24	"	Boat Howitzers,	. . .	"	6,502
2	12	"	Rifled Guns,	. . . .	James,	3,180
2	12	"	Field Guns, Light,	Rebel trophies,	2,400
1	18	"	Gun, Austrian,	.	" trophy,	2,514
			Total, ...			77,493

The next step of Colonel Wilson was the issue of this

CIRCULAR.

Headquarters U. S. Military Academy,
West Point, N. Y., October 29, 1889.

About a quarter of a century ago a number of officers and enlisted men, together with a few citizens, subscribed for a Battle Monument to be erected at West Point, in memory of the officers and enlisted men of the Regular Army who fell in the defense of the Union during the late war.

Of the seven or eight hundred officers who subscribed only about one hundred and sixty still remain in the Army.

The fund now amounts to $50,300.00 in United States Bonds, the value of which, if sold to-day, would be about $63,000.00.

The Superintendent of the Military Academy finds himself, ex officio, President of the Battle Monument Association.

It certainly seems as if action in this matter should no longer be delayed, and that some use should be made of the fund before all of the subscribers shall have passed away.

The Military Academy Chapel is too small, and its present condition — for lack of means to improve it — is not creditable to the Academy. A larger place of worship is needed, and also a hall where important ceremonies can take place, similar to those incident to the recent presentation of portraits.

The Superintendent suggests either the enlargement of the present Chapel, and placing therein mural tablets in memory of our fallen heroes, or the erection of a memorial hall with similar tablets on Trophy Point.

The views of all surviving subscribers upon the subject are invited.

JOHN M. WILSON, Colonel of Engineers,
President Battle Monument Association.

Out of 60 responses to this Circular now on file the expression of opinion regarding the character of the memorial is as follows:

In favor of a Memorial Hall 25
"   "   " a Monument 16
"   "   " an Addition to Chapel 9
"   "   " a New Chapel 5
            No choice 5

West Point, N. Y., January 16, 1890.

At this time the Executive Committee of the Battle Monument consisted of the following named officers:

Col. John M. Wilson, Supt. M. A., *ex officio*,
President.

Lieut.-Col. H. S. Hawkins, Commandant of
Cadets, *ex officio.*

Prof. Geo. L. Andrews,
Treasurer.

Prof. P. S. Michie,	Prof. Chas. W. Larned,
Prof. E. W. Bass,	Prof. Wm. Winthrop,
Prof. James Mercur,	Surg. H. R. Tilton,
Capt. Geo. McC. Derby,	Lieut. Charles Braden.

And their sentiment being favorable, a meeting was called to decide upon the question of immediate action.

West Point, N. Y., January 22, 1890.

Colonel Wilson briefly stated the object of the meeting and gave a short history of the Battle Monument Association from its organization in 1863 to the present time.

Professor Geo. L. Andrews tendered his resignation as Treasurer of the Association and submitted a statement of the condition of the fund.

Professor Andrews' resignation was accepted and it was unanimously voted to extend the thanks of the Association to Professor Andrews for his services as Treasurer during the past twelve years.

Professor Edgar W. Bass was unanimously elected Treasurer of the Association.

A letter from Major George B. Davis, the former Secretary, was read, giving a brief account of the object of the Association and facts relating to the subscribers to the fund.

After remarks by several of the officers present, the following resolution offered by Major Spurgin was adopted:

Resolved, That the Executive Committee be instructed to carry out the original intention of the subscribers to the fund, or take such action as they may deem expedient.

The following resolution was adopted:

Resolved, That the Treasurer be requested to correspond with the Chief of Ordnance and secure as soon as possible the fifty bronze cannon mentioned in Professor Andrews' report, and which are now stored at the Arsenal on Governor's Island, N. Y.

The Chairman announced that he would call a meeting of the Executive Committee at an early day to act upon the business of erecting a suitable monument.

MEETING OF FEBRUARY 18, 1890.

The meeting called by Colonel Wilson for February 18th marks the first Executive Act of the Association in pursuance of its purpose. The Committee appointed at this meeting formulated a line of action which was subsequently adopted and resulted in the erection of the Battle Monument.

West Point, N. Y., February 18, 1890.

Pursuant to a call by Colonel J. M. Wilson, President, issued February 17, 1890, the Executive Committee of the Battle Monument Association met at the Superintendent's quarters at 7.15 P. M.

Present.

Colonel John M. Wilson, Prof. Jas. Mercur,
Lt.-Col. H. S. Hawkins, Prof. P. S. Michie,
Prof. G. L. Andrews, Prof. C. W. Larned,
Prof. E. W. Bass, Prof. Wm. Winthrop,
Surg. H. R. Tilton.

The Chair stated that the object of the meeting was to take preliminary steps towards inviting designs for the Battle Monument to be erected at West Point, N. Y.

After informal discussion, on motion of Professor Bass, a committee was appointed by the Chair to consider and prepare a circular, or to determine what other action might be preferable, in order to invite designs for the monument; it was understood that the members of this Committee would personally consult, upon their next visit to New York, with distinguished sculptors, etc., as to the best method of procedure in the matter.

The Chair appointed as the Committee:

Prof. P. S. Michie,   Prof. C. W. Larned,
Prof. E. W. Bass.

There being no further business before the Committee, the meeting adjourned at 8.15 P. M.

John M. Wilson, Colonel of Engineers,
President of Association.

Charles Braden,
Secretary.

Subsequent to the foregoing meeting the following authorization was received from the Adjutant-General:

War Department,
Adjutant-General's Office,
Washington, February 21st, 1890.

Sir:

Your communication of the 20th instant, concerning the erection at West Point, by the Battle Monument Association, of a Monument to the memory of the officers and enlisted men of the Regular Army of the U. S. who were killed or died of wounds received in action during the war of the rebellion, has been laid before the Secretary of War, who instructs me to inform you that the Association is granted permission to proceed with the work of erecting a monument on Trophy Point.

     Very respectfully,
      J. C. KELTON,
        Adjutant-General.

The Superintendent,
 U. S. Military Academy,
  West Point, N. Y.

The minutes of the next meeting give the report of the sub-committee outlining a method of procedure which governed future action.

West Point, N. Y., March 8, 1890.

Pursuant to the call of the President, the Executive Committee met at 7.30 P. M. to-day, in the Superintendent's quarters.

Present all the members of the Committee, except Surgeon Tilton and Captain Derby.

The minutes of the last meeting were read and approved.

Surgeon Henry McElderry was elected a member of the Executive Committee in place of Surgeon Tilton, relieved from duty at West Point.

The Committee appointed at the meeting held February 18 being called upon for a report, the following was read by Professor Larned:

Report of the Committee of the Battle Monument Association appointed to prepare a plan of procedure.

Your Committee, after some consideration of the matter intrusted to them, concluded to visit New York and seek the advice of sculptors and architects of established reputation. A consultation with Mr. Augustus St. Gaudens, the leading sculptor of America, confirmed the Committee in its opinion that the conditions governing the erection of this Monument, *i. e.*, the number of individuals commemorated by it, the conspicuous nature of the site, and the limited funds available, require that it should be mainly architectural in its character, and that the sculptural features should be subordinate or accessory. A single figure or group of figures of life size would be, in such a place and for such a purpose, inadequate, unless placed upon a pediment or substructure of considerable dimensions, which would also be necessitated by the commemorative inscriptions. So placed, the statuary would appear insignificant unless of heroic size, in which case the cost would be largely beyond the limit of our resources. An architectural structure, however, of such dimensions as to be dignified, and accord with the surroundings, with sculptural accessories in the round or in relief, and decorative tablets, can be erected within the specified amount.

An examination of the results of many public and general competitions shows that they rarely if ever give satisfaction either to the competitors or their clients, and that the feeling is so strong against them among architects of high reputation that they generally decline to enter them. This is due largely to the fact that they are forced to bring their labor and reputations into competition with those of inferior men, and to submit to the judgment of incompetent critics. In a private and selected competition properly conducted, these objections can be avoided, to the great saving of time and friction and with a great gain in the standard of result. Your Committee, therefore, conclude it wise to recommend the adoption of the method of private and selected competition, and to choose for such competition, with proper advice, three or four of the architectural firms of the country having the highest artistic reputation.

With these convictions your Committee visited the office of Messrs. Babb, Cook and Willard, the leading member of the firm having been most highly indorsed by Mr. St. Gaudens as perhaps the most talented of our architects, and laid before these gentlemen the commission intrusted to it, with the request that they would advise as to the course most likely to give the most satisfactory results to all concerned. These gentlemen consented to draw up, after sufficient time for consultation, a memorandum embodying the more important features of such a competition, and to forward it to your Committee. This they have done, and upon this outline as a basis your Committee has prepared the accompanying scheme for your approval.

It, therefore, recommends for adoption the following resolution:

Resolved. 1st. That the Monument shall be mainly architectural in character, with such sculptural accessories as shall be deemed fitting and appropriate by the designer.

2d. That it shall afford proper space for the necessary inscriptions commemorative of its purpose.

3d. That it shall be of sufficient height to give dignity to its proportions, and to harmonize with its surroundings; but that its height shall not be a feature of the design, as in the case of a large column or shaft.

4th. That it be located upon Trophy Point, upon a site to be selected by the Building Committee of this Association, of which the Superintendent of the Military Academy and the successful competitor shall be, for this purpose, members **ex** officio.

5th. That the designer shall be chosen by private selected competition.

6th. That for this purpose four of the architectural firms of this country having high professional reputation shall be invited to compete.

7th. That a Building Committee be appointed consisting of four members of the Executive Committee, which Building Committee shall be authorized to make all necessary arrangements for such competition, to decide upon the merits of the design, and to supervise, with the Superintendent of the Military Academy, its erection, the Superintendent becoming for this purpose, ex officio, a member of the Committee, and its Chairman.

8th. That the Building Committee be authorized to draw upon the Treasurer of this Association for all necessary funds, and to audit all the accounts arising from the disbursements connected with the work, and to take any and all steps necessary to its completion.

9th. That, upon the completion of the Monument, the Building Committee — the Superintendent being, ex officio, a member thereof — shall arrange for proper dedication exercises and ceremonies.

10th. That, upon the selection of the accepted design, a meeting of the Association shall be called and the drawings exhibited.

11th. That, upon dedication, the Monument shall be presented to the Military Academy of the United States, and shall upon acceptance be turned over to the proper military authorities.

12th. That, upon the completion of these duties, the Building Committee shall turn over to the authorities of the Military Academy all vouchers and papers relating to its functions and the action of the Battle Monument Association for file with the records of the Military Academy, and shall be discharged from these functions.

13th. That the Superintendent be requested to obtain from the authorities at Washington the necessary names and data for inscription upon the monument.

   Peter S. Michie, Prof., U. S. M. A.
   Chas. W. Larned, " "
   Edg. W. Bass, " "

Professor Larned, at the request of the Chairman of the Committee, described the action of the Committee in its visit to New York, and after some explanatory remarks and an informal discussion submitted the following form for an invitation to compete for the erection of the monument:

INVITATION TO COMPETE FOR A MONUMENT TO BE ERECTED AT WEST POINT, N. Y.

I.

This Monument is to commemorate the Officers and Soldiers of the Regular Army killed in the War of the Rebellion. It is to be erected upon the land of the Government reservation at West Point, N. Y., the site being that portion of the plain in

front of Cadet Barracks commonly known as Trophy Point; the exact spot to be hereafter designated.

II.

The general character of the design is to be architectural with such sculptural accessories as the taste of the designer may deem fitting and appropriate. It is to be of such proportions as to provide for the display of bronze tablets sufficient in number and dimensions for the inscription of the names of officers and the designation by number and regiment of non-commissioned officers and privates.

The material is to be stone and bronze, the nature of the stone being optional with the designer.

III.

The funds available for this construction, proper, are $50,000 in cash. There are, also, at the disposal of the Association fifty (50) bronze cannon which may be employed in any way deemed proper, presented for the purpose by the following Joint Resolution of Congress:

> *Joint Resolution (No. 37), approved April* 28, 1870.
>
> *Resolved,* &c., &c., &c., That the Secretary of War is hereby authorized and directed to deliver to Professor A. E. CHURCH, Treasurer of the Battle Monument Committee, fifty bronze guns captured from the rebels, to be used in the construction of a monument at West Point, New York, in memory of the officers and soldiers of the regular army who fell in the late war, and in the ornamentation of the grounds around said monument.— 16 *Stats. at Large,* 373.

IV.

You are invited to submit to this Committee of the Battle Monument Association at West Point a design for the above described monument in competition with those of the following named firms of architects :

on or before September 15th, 1890, under the following conditions :

V.

CONDITIONS.

1st. The design to be shown in the following drawings :

1. A Perspective view in color or mono-tint, at your option, on a sheet not smaller than 34×48 inches, in proper relative proportion.

2. A Plan.

3. Elevation of the principal front to scale of $1''$ to $4'$ in line.

Should any of the other fronts possess special features of importance, separate elevations in pencil to same scale showing these features should be submitted with principal drawings.

Each drawing is to be marked with a motto or device, and the whole sent in a sealed package, accompanied by a sealed envelope containing name, and marked with device on outside, to the chairman of this Committee, Professor PETER S. MICHIE, U. S. Military Academy, West Point, N. Y. A complete description of the design with explanation of its material and construction should accompany the drawings.

2d. For the purpose of selection only, the Committee will associate with itself three gentlemen — sculptors or architects — to be chosen from a list of names submitted by the competitors themselves, each competitor submitting three, not more than one to be taken from the list of any one firm. These associates for the purpose named shall each have a full vote, and the result of the vote shall be decisive as to the selection or rejection of the designs submitted.

3d. No designs other than those submitted by the firms named in the list above given shall be admitted in this competition, nor shall any designs from any source be considered by the Committee until after the decision in this instance. After the decision the rejected designs will be returned to their respective owners, and no use in any way will be made of them or any of their features unless by arrangement with and consent of the owner.

The accepted design is to become the property of the Association, and the construction of the monument is to be in the hands and under the direction of the successful competitor, who shall be responsible for its proper and satisfactory completion according to the terms of the detailed specifications and drawings accepted.

It shall be the right of the Superintendent of the Military Academy to appoint a competent officer who shall inspect the work during its progress, and who shall have the power, by direction of the Superintendent, to require a conformity in all particulars with the requirements of the specifications. He shall have the right, as above, to stop work at any stage of progress should he discover any failure on the part of contractors to fulfil such requirements, until the architect can enforce them. His function shall not be construed to interfere in any way with the freedom of action of the architect, or of any person deputed by him to represent him as supervisor or clerk of the work.

The sum of two hundred and fifty dollars ($250.00) will be paid to each competitor as a compensation for time and labor in the preparation of the designs submitted in competition, except that the successful competitor shall receive the usual compensation of 5 per cent. upon the total cost of the monument, which sum shall include cost of all drawings prepared by him.

Should the nature of the design involve special sculptural features requiring separate and original designing by the architects, special arrangements for compensation will be made.

Sculptural designs not furnished by architect must be contracted for by him, and paid out of the fund for general cost of monument as part of the regular expenses.

4th. The design must be carefully calculated to come within the limits of the amount available for construction, as the cost of the monument *can in no case exceed* fifty thousand dollars, exclusive of the value of the bronze guns. To this end an estimate of cost should accompany each design, and upon acceptance a detailed estimate of cost must be submitted to this **Committee**. Should any excess result in this detailed estimate, or in the bids for construction, the design must be so modified as to come within the required limits.

5th. The Committee reserve the right to reject all designs under the conditions of payment and return, as specified above.

6th. For the purpose of definitely locating the site only, the Superintendent of the Military Academy and the successful competitor shall become ex-officio members of the Building Committee, and for the purpose of superintending the construction after selection, and the final arrangements for dedication, the Superintendent of the Military Academy becomes a member of the Committee ex officio, and its Chairman.

VI.

The Committee herein referred to consists of the following named officers of the Military Academy :

>Professor Peter S. Michie, *Chairman*.
>Professor Charles W. Larned.
>Professor Edgar W. Bass, *Treas. Battle Mon. Ass.*
>Professor James Mercur.

They are appointed by authority of the Executive Committee of the Battle Monument Association.

This Association has invested the Executive Committee with full powers for the expenditure of the funds herein de-

scribed, and for the determination of all matters pertaining to the erection of this monument. It has delegated to this Committee authority for action in the premises as above described, and all communications relative to the matter in hand will be addressed to it through its Chairman, Professor Peter S. Michie.

An informal discussion took place, after which the report of the Committee was accepted, and the Committee discharged from further action.

The sections were discussed and considered in detail. All were adopted as submitted, except No. 3, which was amended to mean that the principal view should be "as seen from the plain."

The following resolution was adopted:

Resolved. That the Superintendent be requested to name a committee of four to take charge of the building of the Monument, and that after the Committee is appointed and vacancies occur, the other members of the Committee be authorized to fill said vacancies.

In pursuance of this resolution, the following were appointed members of the Committee: Professor Michie, Professor Larned, Professor Bass and Professor Mercur.

It was moved and carried that the Committee prepare and send a circular letter to competitors.

The following resolution was adopted:

That the Building Committee can change the specifications as it thinks proper, keeping the general idea of the Monument in view at all times.

* * * * * *

After careful investigation and consultation the following named firms of architects were selected for the competition and a circular letter inclosing a printed copy of the terms of competition was addressed to them by the Secretary of the Building Committee: Babb, Cook & Willard, New York City; Carrere & Hastings, New York City; McKim, Mead & White, New York City; and R. W. Emerson, Boston, Mass. The circular letter contained the following paragraphs:

The history of the action of which this proposed competition is the outcome is briefly as follows:

During the War of the Rebellion certain officers of the regular army stationed at West Point conceived the idea of commemorating their brother officers of the regular army killed in that struggle by a monument erected there, and to that end formed an association known as the Battle Monument Association, with headquarters at the Military Academy. Letters were sent out to all officers of the regular army inviting contributions in proportion to the rate of pay received. The fund resulting was placed in the custody of the Treasurer of the Association, invested in government bonds, and has increased through accrued interest to its present size. Congress was petitioned to further the project by appropriating a certain number of bronze cannon, and acceded by placing at the disposal of the Association fifty bronze guns captured from the

rebels. It was proposed to make the monument commemorative as well of the non-commissioned officers and privates, which proposition was adopted with the proviso that the description should be by number and regiment only. The Executive Committee of the above described Association, in which was invested plenary power both to act and to expend the funds accrued, in turn has transferred its authority to a Building Committee from which this circular emanates, and which purposes to push the project to completion. This monument, therefore, is distinctly commemorative of the officers, non-commissioned officers and privates of the regular army of the United States killed, or who died of wounds received in action, during the War of the Rebellion.

In regard to the bronze guns available for use in the work, the committee desires it to be understood that they are at the disposition of the architect *en masse*, to be used to defray the cost in a finished state of all bronze decorations used upon the monument. In other words, the committee conceives it to be a legitimate use of this material to employ it not only as material, but to defray the cost of its own working and designing. Should, however, the cost of working exceed the value of the guns, the excess will be paid from the general fund. It will follow therefore that the bronze decorations should be a considerable feature of the design in order that all of the guns shall be available for use. As these guns are in themselves commemorative and historic, the committee suggests that a certain number of them — say ten or more — be retained intact for direct decoration in the monument, or as accessories on the plinth and stylobate, or in the grounds in the immediate neighborhood.

The invitation to compete was identical with the form adopted as given above, and, after formal acceptance on the part of the firms addressed, their members were invited to visit West Point as the guests of the Building Committee to inspect the site, and an exact location was determined on by a general vote of the Committee and the competitors. As the date of competition matured, a selection of associates was made by the Building Committee from the list of candidates nominated by the competitors. These associates became, for the purpose of choice, members of the Committee with a full vote, and the action of this jury was final. The names of these gentlemen, who at once most courteously consented to serve, are R. M. Hunt, President American Institute of Architects; Augustus St. Gaudens; Arthur Rotch.

On the date of competition they were invited, as guests of the Building Committee, to visit West Point, where the jury proceeded to examine the drawings. After a long and careful study, a final vote resulted in the selection of the design marked "Monolith"— the motto of the firm of McKim, Mead & White. The results of the competition were very gratifying, and the merits of all the designs so conspicuous as to render final decision a matter of nice discrimination based upon many considerations.

Messrs. McKim, Mead & White made the following statement regarding their design:

> In preparing the design, we have most carefully considered the object of the monument and the site which it is to occupy.

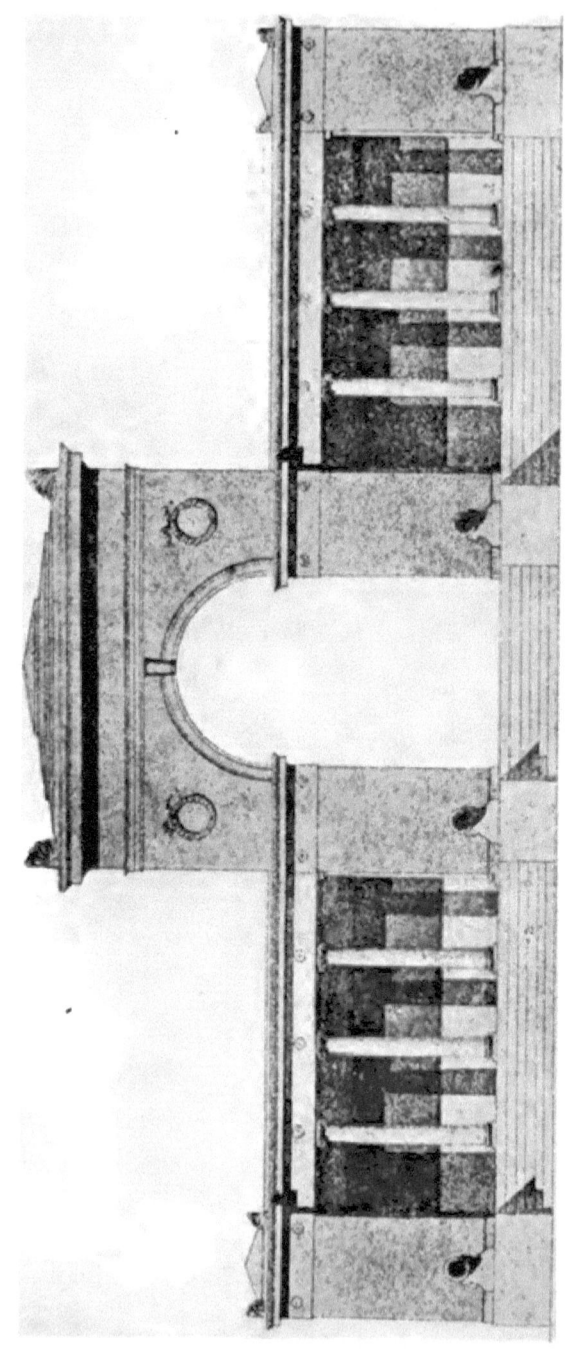

We believe the monument should be first and foremost a martial one, distinctive in its character and impressive in its design. The beauty of its site and the surroundings seems to us to preclude any bulky or massive treatment, and to suggest rather a treatment where the impression should be produced by height supported by a base which should not interfere with graceful and artistic treatment. For this reason we have adopted as the feature of our design a single monolithic shaft treated in the shape of a memorial column, or column of victory. This form seems to us to be more distinctively martial than any other, and in this form we believe it is possible to obtain impressiveness and dignity without a sacrifice of grace, at the same time preserving a distinctively architectural and monumental character. We lay great stress upon these two points, viz.: the necessity of giving the monument a martial character, and the relation of the monument to its site. In our design we have had these two points continually in mind, with results which you must judge. The shaft is a monolith of polished granite forty-six feet high and five feet six inches in diameter. To the best of our belief, it would be the largest polished shaft in the world. It is proposed to surmount it with a figure of Victory, and surround it by eagles — a distinct mark of its national character. The shaft rests upon a circular base, surrounded by flights of steps, giving the greatest breadth and dignity possible to the base. The materials are the most enduring — granite and bronze.

We have received an estimate from the most reliable firm known to us upon this monument which comes within the amount available. We submit with this statement a memorandum specification and copy of this bid.

Very respectfully,
"Monolith."

MEMORANDUM OF ESTIMATED COST OF PROPOSED BATTLE MONUMENT.

Messrs. Norcross Bros.' estimate for granite work,	$41,000.00
Our estimate for figure, ...	5,000.00
Our estimate for eagles, ...	4,000.00
	$50,000.00
Value of bronze cannon to cover architects' fees and contingencies	5,000.00

The designs of the other competing firms are shown in the half-tone prints in this report.

The contract for the erection of the monument was let to Messrs. Norcross Bros., of New York City, and the sculptor for the figure of Fame surmounting the shaft, selected by Messrs. McKim, Mead & White and approved by the Building Committee, was Mr. Frederick MacMonnies. The architects desired to make some modifications in the design, and were permitted to do so, the most notable change from the accepted design being the omission of the eagles surrounding the shaft. Owing to various delays incident to changes and modifications of details, the procuring and correction of the lists of names of officers and men, and their casting in bronze tablets, the work progressed somewhat slowly. Instead of the site dedicated by General McClellan in 1864, a new site contiguous to it was selected by the architect and Building

Committee to the east of Trophy Point, and about midway between it and the hotel.

This site is a very conspicuous one from the river, and this consideration largely determined its selection.

The quarrying, transportation and erection of so large a mass as the monolithic shaft — probably the largest polished monolith in the world — are matters of considerable difficulty, requiring very great caution and considerable engineering skill; and the details of the operations involved are fully described in a separate section.

By the spring of 1894, the shaft was ready to receive the figure of Fame, and accordingly it was placed in position facing toward the Library Building. It was hoped that the monument would be completed and in readiness for dedication by October of this year, and partial preparations for the dedication ceremonies were made. In the meanwhile formal criticism of the figure of Fame, involving its replacement, having been made by a member of the Committee and acquiesced in by the architect, it was decided that the figure must be replaced. Ultimately the architect offered to assume the entire expense of this change, and a new figure was undertaken at once by Mr. MacMonnies. As a necessary consequence, the dedication was postponed and May 31, 1895, selected for the event. Before that time it became evident that completion could not be hoped for until later, and the matter was left for future decision. Great difficulty was experienced in securing correctness in the casting of the bronze tablets, and many alterations were demanded before their completion and location on the monument. The lists of names had been carefully prepared in the office of the Adjutant-General of the Army, and afterwards were examined critically by both the Chairman of the Committee and the Treasurer. The lists and tablets were repeatedly checked after casting, and everything done to insure accuracy in the record.

Early in May, 1896, the new figure was put in place, but various modifications in the details of the monument and the location of the bronzes rendered it impossible to dedicate in June, as the Committee had hoped to do. It was not until March, 1897, that definite steps were taken to arrange for the final ceremonies and the date fixed for May 31st. It was decided to make the event memorable, and, after careful consultation, a list of those to whom invitations were to be extended was prepared. This list is as follows:

The President of the United States;
The Vice-President of the United States;
Members of the Cabinet of the President of the United States;
The Chief Justice of the Supreme Court;
The Speaker of the House of Representatives;
The General of the Army and all officers of the Regular Army;
Graduates of the United States Military Academy;
Architects, Sculptor and Competing Architects;

Members of the Selection Committee;
Veterans of the Regular Army who served in the War of the Rebellion;
Families of Soldiers commemorated by Monument;
The Commander of the Loyal Legion;
The Commander of the Grand Army;
The Superintendent and Officers of the Naval Academy;
Heads of Bureaus of the Naval Department.

The invitation was the subject of much careful consideration, and was printed from special type originally cast in Philadelphia in the 18th century. It consisted of four leaves on heavy rough paper with uncut edges, tinted pale buff. On the first or cover page was an artotype of the figure of Fame; on the 3d page the invitation in black and red ink; on the 5th an artotype of the monument; on the 7th the names of the Building Committee and Architects; on the 8th or rear cover was printed the order of the exercises. A special card entitling the holder to a seat was sent with each invitation, the assignment being made upon presentation of this card at the Auditorium.

The wording of the invitation was as follows, the letters in italics being in red ink:

1st page.
The Dedication Ceremonies of the
Battle Monument at West Point,
[Figure of Fame.]
The thirty-first day of May,
MD CCC XC VII.

THE BATTLE MONUMENT

3d page.

THE honor of your presence is requested at West Point, New York, on Monday, May the thirty-first, eighteen hundred and ninety-seven, at half after eleven o'clock, at the dedication of the BATTLE MONUMENT erected in memory of the Officers and Men of the *Regular Army of the United States* who fell in battle during the *War of the Rebellion* by their surviving comrades.

In behalf of the *Building Committee,*
Charles W. Larned, *Professor United States Military Academy,* Secretary.

THE favor of an early reply is earnestly requested.

7th page.

The Building Committee.

Colonel Oswald H. Ernst, *Corps of Engineers, United States Army, Superintendent of the United States Military Academy,* Chairman, *ex officio.*

Professor Peter S. Michie, *United*

States Military Academy, Brevet Lieutenant-Colonel United States Army.

Professor Charles W. Larned, *United States Military Academy*, Secretary.

Professor Edgar W. Bass, *United States Military Academy*, Treasurer.

Colonel John M. Wilson, *Corps of Engineers, United States Army, Superintendent of the Military Academy*, Chairman *Ex-officio* from 1890 to 1893.

Professor James Mercur, *United States Military Academy*, from 1890 to 1896, deceased.

Professor Albert E. Church, *United States Military Academy*, Treasurer from 1864 to 1878, deceased.

Professor George L. Andrews, *United States Military Academy*, from 1878 to 1890, resigned.

McKim, Mead and White, Architects, Frederick W. MacMonnies, Sculptor.

8*th page.*

The Order *of the* Exercises.

Music by the *Band* of the *Military Academy.*

A Prayer by Reverend Herbert Shipman,
Chaplain of the *Military Academy.*

Presentation to the *United States Army* by Brigadier-General John M. Wilson, *Chief of Engineers, United States Army.*

Acceptance by Lieutenant-General John M. Schofield, *Retired*, and Presentation to the *General Government.*

Acceptance by the *President of the United States.*

The National Salute.

The Star Spangled Banner by the *Band* of the *Military Academy.*

Oration by the Honorable David J. Brewer, Associate Justice of the *Supreme Court* of the *United States.*

Handel's Largo by the *Band* of the *Military Academy.*

Benediction *by* Reverend Herbert Shipman, *Chaplain* of the *Military Academy.*

DEDICATION CEREMONIES
AT
WEST POINT

DEDICATION CEREMONIES AT WEST POINT.

THE morning of the dedication opened wet and threatening, with heavy cloud mists and showers. By ten o'clock, however, the sun broke through the clouds with a superb effect of light and shade, and the ceremonies took place without interruption, although the threatening weather kept away a large number of those who would otherwise have attended. The President of the United States had delegated his function in the ceremony to the Secretary of War, who, together with Lieutenant-General J. M. Schofield, formerly Commanding the Army; Brigadier-General J. M. Wilson, Chief of Engineers; and Justice D. J. Brewer, of the Supreme Court of the United States, had arrived on the previous day. The Corps of Cadets were marched under arms to the Auditorium and occupied seats in rear. The members of the distinguished party who were to take part in the ceremonies were escorted in carriages by the Superintendent and members of the Academic Board to the rostrum, which was occupied also by others of conspicuous rank or service.

The circular grand stand, designed by the architect to accommodate over a thousand spectators, faced a raised rostrum, both covered by awnings of red and white striped canvas decorated with flags and trophies, the whole forming a very brilliant and beautiful mass of color. The ceremonies opened with prayer by the Chaplain of the Military Academy and the regular order of the programme was followed without change other than that of the substitution by the President of the United States, who was unable to be present, of the Secretary of War as his representative.

OPENING PRAYERS.

I. The Lord's Prayer.

II. God of heaven and earth, who leddest our fathers forth, making them go from one kingdom to another people; we yield Thee hearty thanks for all that Thou didst for them and art doing for the land to which they came. We remember that their communion was to eat their bread in exile, their sacrament to shed their blood for others. And we give Thee thanks for them. In particular, we remember here and now those of a later day who spared not their lives that our land might be one; patriots of the newer time; prophets and martyrs of our country's unity and peace. And for them we give Thee thanks. And we pray that we may follow their good examples and bequeath to those that come after a nation worthy of its founders and preservers, a nation fitted and glad to do Thy will, a nation subject alone to Thee and to Thy Christ. May the memory of those who offered up their lives for principle, for unity in which alone peace could be, lift and draw the coming generations upward and forward to see and seek that true and perfect peace which Thou willest for all the sons of men. May we feel and heed the silent yet solemn protest, rising from the graves of those who died for their country's honor and integrity, against all that is untrue, unworthy of the high and holy destiny we believe Thou hast set before this nation.

May we, like them, placing before the love of self, the love of others; before the love of earthly gain and life itself, the love of truth and righteousness; bring nearer that day, for which Thy Son's last earthly prayer went up, when all Thy children shall be one in love. We ask this in Thy Name, O Heavenly Father; in Thine, O blessed Son, who art the Prince of Peace; in Thine, O Holy Spirit, who guidest the hearts and minds of men in the way of light and truth; in thine, O One Eternal God, to whom be dominion, power and glory, now and forever. Amen.

ADDRESS OF GENERAL WILSON.

MR. Chairman, Ladies and Gentlemen:

That hero, statesman, and martyr, Abraham Lincoln, in his grand inaugural, expressed the exquisite sentiment that, "The mystic chords of memory, stretching from every battle-field and patriot's grave to every living heart and hearthstone all over this broad land, will yet swell the chorus of the Union, when touched, as they surely will be, by the better angels of our nature."

May I not borrow this glowing language to-day and say that the mystic chords of memory, stretching from the Maine mosaic block of the Union to the coral reefs of Florida, from the orange groves of Louisiana to the ice palaces of Minnesota, from the vine-clad hills of Southern California to the majestic forests of Puget Sound, are joined in one grand electric circuit within which, at every hearthstone from which a soldier departed to fill a patriot's grave, hearts are throbbing and pulses tingling at the thought that to-day, upon this historic spot, will be dedicated a monument erected in memory of the heroes of the regular army who gave up their lives in the defense of the honor of the nation and the perpetuity of the Union.

More than a third of a century ago, a few noble and gallant officers, who had been sent to duty at this post, some of whom were slowly recovering from wounds received in action, and others who were convalescing from the fearful fevers contracted in the Chickahominy swamps, conceived the idea of erecting, at West Point, a monument to the memory of the officers and enlisted men of the regular army who had fallen in the terrible conflict then in progress, and to others who might give up their lives in the cause of the nation.

At the suggestion of that splendid soldier, that courteous and accomplished gentleman, that much loved comrade, Col. Henry C. Hasbrouck, of the 4th Artillery, then a young lieutenant of artillery, a meeting of the officers was called, an Executive Committee constituted, and circulars sent to the commanding generals of the army and to others, outlining the object in view and soliciting coöperation.

The replies surpassed the most ardent anticipations, and the committee, realizing that it could act in the name of the army, prepared and distributed to their comrades in the field and elsewhere circulars inviting subscriptions.

The beloved and lamented Professor A. E. Church was appointed treasurer, and during the year 1864 over $14,000 was received, the grand total eventually reaching, by 1871, the sum of $14,856.54, after which no further subscriptions were received.

This amount was subscribed by 670 officers, 790 enlisted men and civilian employees representing all branches of the regular service and the civil employees of the Quartermaster's Department at New Orleans.

Among the subscribers were Generals Grant, Sheridan, Meade, Thomas, Buell, Foster, Franklin, French, Gillmore, Heintzelman, Hitchcock, Hooker, Howard, Keyes, McCook, McDowell, Parke, Pope, Reynolds, Rosecrans, Sedgwick, Slocum, Steele, Sykes, Warren, Webb, and Wright.

A site was selected and dedicated for the monument on June 15, 1864, the oration having been delivered by that distinguished soldier, the late Major-Gen. Geo. B. McClellan.

For some reason not fully understood by us, the matter languished, the actual construction of the monument was postponed, and the meetings of the Executive Committee became exceedingly rare, only four or five having been recorded between October, 1864, and January, 1890.

In the meantime the grand old treasurer had not buried the talent committed to his charge, but by skilful management the fund had been so invested that upon his death in 1878 it had been increased to about $32,000.

Professor Church was succeeded by Professor Geo. L. Andrews, of the U. S. Military Academy, a distinguished officer of the army during the war, who was equally successful in his stewardship; and when he resigned his treasurership early in 1890, he transferred to his successor, our beloved friend Col. E. W. Bass, the eminent professor of mathematics, bonds whose market value at the time was over $60,000.

Early in the year 1890 the subject was again brought forward, and the officers then at the Military Academy, some of whom had not yet seen the light of day when the great conflict was initiated, took up the matter with such enthusiasm that it was finally consummated, and the result is before you.

In addition to the available funds, fifty bronze cannon captured during the war were presented by the War Department, some of which have been placed around the monument, and others used to provide for bronze tablets and ornaments.

A new Executive Committee, consisting of several of the eminent professors of the Academy, was constituted, and this committee, after consultation with distinguished artists, sculptors, and architects in New York, in order to obtain the highest order of art, decided to invite designs from four firms of exalted reputation.

The parties invited, and who promptly and courteously accepted the invitation, were:

Messrs. McKim, Mead and White,
Messrs. Babb, Cook and Willard,
Messrs. Carrère and Hastings, and
Mr. W. R. Emerson.

The results exceeded the highest anticipations of the committee, and the superb designs presented reflected the greatest credit upon the distinguished gentlemen who had competed for the prize.

The Executive Committee, still anxious to make no mistake and to do no injustice, called to its aid, in selecting the design to be accepted, Messrs. Richard M. Hunt, Augustus St. Gaudens, and Arthur Roache, men whose reputations in their profession were second to none others in our broad land.

After most critical examination, and upon the advice of these eminent experts, the design of Messrs. McKim, Mead and White was adopted, the modeling of the figure of Fame which crowns the shaft being intrusted to Mr. Frederick MacMonnies, and the construction of the monument to the Messrs. Norcross Brothers, of Worcester, Mass.

The marvelous creation of these artists, with its exquisite lines, its symmetry and beauty, is before you, and no words that I can utter can do it justice.

It bears upon it the names of 188 officers and 2042 enlisted men; and, through the courtesy of the War Department at Washington, it is believed that the name of every officer and of every enlisted man of the regular army who was killed in action or died of wounds received in action during the great war of 1861–65 is placed in enduring bronze, so that the youths of our land, who are here serving their squirehood in their country's services, may have before them, as an everlasting example, a list of heroes who laid down their lives in the cause of the nation.

Every arm of the service, and every regiment in the service, save one which was not in the field but kept on other important duty during the war, is represented by the names of some of its heroes upon the monument.

Lieutenant-General Schofield, it is meet and right that to-day, through you, one of its most distinguished heroes, this monument should be transferred to the Army of the United States.

To you, our former and beloved commander — to you, the ideal soldier, the heroic commander of many a well-fought and victorious field, the soldier *sans peur et sans reproche*, alike at home in the din of battle or the councils of the nation, whose brilliant stars were won in a baptism of fire,— it is my duty, my pleasure, and my pride, in the name of the Building Committee, to transfer this wonderful work of the genius of man.

The polished granite sphere which surmounts the beautiful shaft is symbolic of the well-rounded lives of the heroes who have been called before the Great White Throne, and I believe that he who lays down his life in the defense of his country's honor is received by the King of kings with those joyous words: "Well done, thou good and faithful servant: thou hast been faithful over a few things, I will make thee ruler over many things: enter thou into the joy of thy Lord."

Capping the whole of this grand work is MacMonnies' ideal creation of Fame; and while we admire its wondrous beauty, as it holds forth the chaplet of victory for these heroes, there come to our mind those glowing words of O'Hara:

> "On Fame's eternal camping-ground
> Their silent tents are spread,
> And Glory guards with solemn round
> The bivouac of the dead."

ADDRESS OF GENERAL SCHOFIELD.

THE purest patriotism is that which inspires the simple soldier, who, of his own choice, offers his services and his life to execute the orders of the Commander-in-Chief. He looks to the head of the nation alone for the national will. The President's policy is his policy, the President's orders his only rule of action. He eliminates self absolutely from his motives, and learns to be content with hunger, privation, hardship, wounds, and death in the effort to execute the orders of the Commander-in-Chief. He is not only willing to die for his country, but he accepts without question or doubt the choice made by his countrymen of the leader whose orders he is to obey and whose policy he is to accept as the will of the nation. This is the purest example of patriotic devotion of which man is capable, and that which the true soldier most highly honors.

It is the just and proud boast of the armies of the United States that this has always been their standard of patriotic duty, and in this the difference between the regular and volunteer exists only in name. The one, no less than the other, is a volunteer soldier, and the other, hardly less than the first, soon becomes, under the discipline of war, a regular soldier. The sublimest fact in American history is the perfect discipline, patient endurance, undoubting confidence of final triumph even in the midst of temporary defeat, and heroic valor shown by our soldiers during four years of war. They knew little and cared less about the dissensions among politicians over questions of public policy, or the troubles of financiers over the state of the treasury. They fought bravely on as they were led, with no thought but the triumph of the Union cause as the end of their soldierly duty.

In all this soldierly devotion there was little room for difference of rank. Only a very few of the highest commanders were at liberty to indulge in other thoughts. With such few exceptions, soldiers of all grades, from the private in the ranks to the general in command of a division or army corps, were governed by the same devotion, obedience, faith, and courage.

These are the patriotic qualities which soldiers honor in their comrades, and especially in those who have given their lives in the country's service. As the States of the Union, and the regiments which they sent to the field, and the various corps of the great Union army have erected fitting monuments in honor of their heroic dead, so the little body of regulars contributed during the war a generous fund for the purpose of erecting here, on this historic spot, a monument to their fallen comrades. That work was delayed, if my memory is not at fault, in order that the increase due to judicious investment might in no very long time enable the trustees to erect a monument much more appropriate to the purpose and the place than could at first have been done.

The wisdom and fidelity with which this sacred trust has been discharged is fully attested by the beautiful and noble work of art now presented to us. In the name of the army, I thank all who have taken part in this noble work for the fidelity with which they have discharged the trust reposed in them.

And in behalf of the army I accept from the Building Committee this Battle Monument, as a worthy token of our respect and reverence for the memories of our comrades who gave their lives to preserve the national Union.

Let every young soldier who shall here follow in the footsteps of these heroes be inspired, as he looks upon this monument, by a noble ambition to so master the art of war that he shall neither live nor die in vain, and so fit himself for his patriotic duty that in his life, as in his death, he shall be an honor to his country.

To you, Mr. Secretary, comrade in battle of the brave men whose names are engraved hereon, I now present this monument, in memory of our fallen heroes, and place it, through you, in the custody of the National Government. Let it and the ground on which it stands be held sacred forever.

ADDRESS OF
THE SECRETARY OF WAR.

GENERAL SCHOFIELD: By command of the President, in whose name I appear to-day, I accept for the Government of the United States this beautiful monument erected to her honored dead. It will stand a lasting memento to those men who gave their lives to save this nation from destruction when the question of its existence was given over to the arbitrament of arms. This is the fittest spot in the land for its abiding-place. Here is the soldier school of the republic, famed for the classic beauty of its surroundings, and sanctified by its association with the names of men whose genius and valor in defense of the government which educated them to the profession of arms, and whose loyalty to the flag which here in their early manhood they were taught to love, have brought imperishable renown to the country of their devotion. This, too, is the fittest day of all the year for its unveiling and dedication, for it is the day set apart by the people and by the law for popular tribute to those who on land and sea offered their lives a willing sacrifice upon the altar of loyalty and liberty. It is pleasant to remember, as we gaze for the first time upon this graceful shaft, that every Union soldier's grave within reach of our people has been strewn by loving hands with beautiful flowers, and it is sweet to fancy that the graves unmarked and unknown, scattered throughout the land wherever soldiers fought and died, are not left unadorned by the kindly hand of nature.

It will be ever gladly borne in mind that this monument does not simply commemorate the names and fame of those who wore the insignia of rank. It rescues and brings out into the light, to share in that way the fame of their commanders, names little known nor much remembered, save in the small circle of home and loved ones. It was quite characteristic of the chivalrous men who planned this memorial to take thought of the humble, but equally devoted and daring, men who followed where they led, and who equally with them, without the spur of ambition or the hope of fame, gave their lives in the line of duty. Had they forgotten, which they could not, the rank and file, without whose discipline, fidelity and bravery there is no fame for a commander, they would have been less the ideal soldiers that they were and less worthy of remembrance, for the true soldier and officer never forgets what he owes to the men he commands.

It is altogether well and worthy that these names of enlisted men are borne upon this monument in one grand muster roll with those of their commanders. Could this shaft, now towering above us, have been builded as high as the deeds of the men in whose memory it is erected deserve, its capstone, indeed, would be lost beyond the skies.

In the history of all nations that which has made them great in prosperity and in strength has been achieved in war, and the brightest of its pages are illumined by the deeds of knightly men in the field. It can truthfully be said that greater disaster can come to a nation than war, for life without honor is not worth the living, and the short span that is given to man, even at its greatest length, is nothing as compared to the sustaining of the dignity and strength of the nation and the keeping alive that patriotism which is so essential to its existence.

Many men have seen war in its terrible aspect, but to none is it given to describe it. War should be but for defense, else Providence were seemingly but the plaything for men's passions. Even to-day the greatest nations of the earth must see its horrors in both hemispheres, regretful that such struggles must come, hopeful that from the conflict may spring a lasting peace. From all people has come the reverence of the most heroic deed that can be performed by mortal man — death in the defense of country, home and faith. Greater far than the glory which crowns the victor, more sublime than tongue can picture him, lies in the dust at the feet of armies, the soldier who served without hope of reward or glory, and fell to be buried and named "Unknown."

Now a word to you young men gathered here to-day, whose profession is war. The spotless integrity of the men who have graduated at this great academy in their official and daily lives is a guide for you, and wherever you may be called, whether in time of peace or armed conflict, remember that you are marked men — the successors of those whose names must live immortal when succeeding generations shall have passed away. Should I name these men the pulse would quicken, and the glory of the old flag they defended would brighten in your thoughts, but you have their example for your beacon light. Go forward then, in life, young men, knowing that you have the prayers and hopes of seventy millions of people with you, and remember that over you floats the proudest flag in the world, that which symbolizes freedom, civilization, Christianity. That flag, glorious in its purity, has never been unfurled in front of any foe but to prevail, nor will it in the time that is to come. That flag shall guard the life of every American in every land and at whatever cost.

Guard well then your heritage, and keep ever before you the thought that patriotism is the highest impulse in the world, that the good that men do always lives, and he who is never swerved by temptation, but stands for the right, wears the crown of American manhood.

It is the fond hope of the best minds of every land that the time may come — and that in the near future — when armed force in the field shall no longer be required, when all differences between nations shall be settled by the benign influences of man's best judgment, and that arbitration shall be substituted for artillery, musketry and the saber. But while man is mortal perhaps the hope that this consummation so devoutly wished may become the rule of the world, cannot be realized, and it is therefore incumbent upon every prudent people to at all times be prepared for any emergency, so that if war should come they would be in readiness.

May we then hope, the soldier equally with the civilian, that the day will come when with one accord the great nations of the earth shall say: "Let the bugler sound the truce of God to the world forever." God speed the coming of that day! In no human heart will that prayer be stronger than in the heart of the true soldier. Remember that "peace hath her victories no less renowned than war," and that the country has use for chivalrous soldiers in peace as well as war.

ADDRESS OF JUSTICE BREWER.

IT is one of the paradoxes of life that that which to eye and touch seems solid and enduring will assuredly crumble and disappear, while that which the eye and touch cannot reach is alone immortal. There is no work of man wrought on canvas, in marble or bronze, lifted in column or cathedral, but soon or late yields up its form and beauty as time's unceasing pendulum is swung by Him with whom a thousand years are as one day, and one day as a thousand years. While on the other hand those viewless, intangible things, born of the brain and soul, lofty thoughts and heroic purposes, live on and on with all the dewy freshness of unfading youth. "The beings of the mind are not of clay; essentially immortal."

Phidias and Praxiteles chiseled their dreams of beauty into the solid marble, singing as they wrought,

"For art can grant what love denies,
And fix the fugitive;"

only broken statues and wretched fragments remain to tell of their forgotten dreams. But the marvelous philosophy of

Plato, the lofty thought of Socrates, the logic of Aristotle, and the epic grandeur of Homer, are as young and inspiring to-day as when first syllabled beneath the groves of the Academy, or chanted through the hamlets of Greece. Nineteen centuries ago the temple of Jerusalem, forty and six years in building, crowned the summit of Mount Moriah as the great achievement of Jewish art, the pride and wonder of the nation. Its ruins are scarcely discoverable, while the loving words of the humble Galilean, spoken beneath the shadow of its glory, are the ever-living comfort and solace of unnumbered millions. The massive Pyramids still stand, and the huge Sphinx still tosses in the face the unsolved riddle of its being, but the broken angles and loosened stones of the former and the battered face of the latter attest their subjection to the crumbling touch of time. Indeed, this whole earth is one mighty sepulcher within which are entombed in hopeless confusion all the beauty and splendor that past generations were able to put into forms of matter, while the only things that preserve the freshness of youth and pass on from age to age with all the vigor and bloom of immortality, are those intangible and viewless things, ideas, feelings — the children of the human soul.

Is the work of the painter, the sculptor and the architect then in vain? Is it idle to paint forms of beauty on the canvas, to chisel them in marble or bronze? Is it a waste of time and labor to lift the columned glory or to put the symmetry and grace of architecture into capitol and cathedral? Is it wrong or foolish to challenge the inexorable law of material decay, to place before the eye the visible beauty which we know must one day disappear? Not so; certainly not, if that thing of matter both carries with it the sweet influences of beauty, and also is eloquent of ideas and purposes which are an inspiration to humanity and will continue so to be long after that which represents them has passed away. While it endures, it incarnates the thought. It is the visible expression of the idea which is itself immortal. And so, as long as it endures, it carries a message to every human soul, and as a carrier of such message deserves the time and labor and money put into it.

We stand to-day in the presence of a stately column, erected by the soldiers and officers of the regular army of the United States, to commemorate the heroism and sacrifice of those of their number who during the civil war gave their lives for their country and in order that "liberty and union might remain now and forever one and inseparable." We are here not simply to speak our praises of its beauty, but more to bow in reverence before the ideas and the ideals which have found material expression in that beauty, and which we believe will be the inspiration not only of this great land but of humanity the world over, long after the column shall have fallen and crumbled into dust. We come, not so much to eulogize it as a work of art, but rather to attest the great fact that brought it into being, and to take a solemn oath in the presence of high heaven that that fact shall never pass from the remembrance of man.

And now what are the ideas and ideals which this column expresses? What are the lessons which, as it stands in solitary grandeur beside the flowing waters of this majestic stream, it teaches to us, and will teach to those who come after us? What is it that this witness, eloquent though mute, says to us, and will say to the generations yet to come? Of the many voices which it bears I have only time to notice two. I know it speaks of heroic achievements. I know it voices the glorious and immortal thought, *dulce et decorum est pro patria mori.* I know it is eloquent with the suffering and self-denial and sacrifice which the great war developed and ennobled. But beyond all that, it bears two voices, which I fain would catch in the words of my talk, and speak to every citizen of the United States.

And first it voices the immeasurable value of law and peace.

It says to us that they whose names are written on its face gave up their lives not merely for military glory, but also that war should cease, and peace with all its blessings prevail ; that every citizen might find the doors of the court-house open for the punishment of wrong and the enforcement of right ; that the humblest might stand side by side with the highest, placing in the ballot-box his equal vote in the settlement of all questions of public policy. They died that a government created by all should not be destroyed by a part, and that, as all once voluntarily consented to its establishment, only in like manner should any change be made in its provisions or any territory released from its dominion. They read in the Constitution the solemn declaration that it and the laws of the United States made in pursuance thereof "shall be the supreme law of the land," and they gave their lives to make that declaration good. It is fitting that in the dedication of this monument there should be heard the voice of a member of the Supreme Court of the United States, the court which the Constitution provided as the ultimate judicial tribunal for the settlement of questions of private right and public law ; for, through the sacrifice and heroism of these illustrious dead it continues still the supreme court for South Carolina and Texas as for New York and Kansas. These men died that law might live, that the will of the people incarnated in constitution and statutes should be obeyed by every one, and that all questions of policy, all disputes as to rights of property, or obligations of contracts, should be settled peaceably in the courts or at the ballot-box. They marched beneath the Stars and Stripes not merely that no star should be dimmed, not merely that its folds might float on the shores of the Gulf of Mexico as well as by the great lakes, but also that so floating triumphantly it should speak to every child of America the comforting words of assured peace and law. On its folds may there ever be seen the words of General Grant, "Let us have peace."

Is this voice worth listening to? In the shadow of the sacred memories which gather around the names of these heroic dead, in the presence of these veterans who yet live to tell the stories of the great war, and in the presence of these eager and enthusiastic youth who are here studying that they may learn all the possibilities of military science, and, whenever duty shall call, win on the battle-field the victor's laurels,— in all this presence I affirm that the greatest meed of praise which can be bestowed upon the army of the United States is, that it makes certain to every citizen the blessings of peace and order and law. Doubtless, young gentlemen, as you look over the bright fields of the future, you see dazzling before you visions of military glory; "the pride, pomp and circumstance of glorious war" are there, and the eagle and the stars wait to rest on your shoulders; but when the evening of life shall come you will realize that the highest praise which can be awarded to you is that in your military lives you have been the defenders of law and the guardians of peace; that you have stood behind the multitudinous business activities of this mighty people, and thundered in the ears of all the irresistible declaration that those activities should go on undisturbed by rebel or mob; that you have been beside the marvelous postal machine which, like a thing of life, reaches its myriad fingers into every city and village and neighborhood, gathering and distributing the sweet messages of love and the rich words of trade; beside the swift-rolling wheels which bear into and through every State the mighty volume of our internal commerce, and bade no man dare to stay the free movement of fingers or wheels; that while the representatives of the people have gathered in the halls of Congress to legislate, the judges have sat on the bench to adjust private rights and public wrongs, and the President has taken his place in the White House to execute the laws and enforce the judgments, you have stood back of legislator and judge and President, and been the unfailing guarantor that in peace they shall act, and that by every citizen their acts shall be respected and obeyed.

There is no true American who does not look with honest pride on the army of the United States, who does not feel his heart thrill with exultation as he repeats the names of its illustrious leaders; there is no true American who would withhold aught that will help to make that army in the future as in the past, though small in numbers, most efficient and potent; there is no true American who depreciates its achievements, or sneers at its usefulness; and yet, while all this is true, every one sees in the organized and disciplined and educated force that which means not war, but peace; that which means not alone military glory, but also the securing to every city and village and home in the land the priceless blessings of law and order. And to-day this column lifts its stately height in the presence of the American people, proclaiming to all, in a voice which fills the land and will fill the centuries, that these men died that law might live and peace prevail.

The other voice which comes from this silently eloquent witness is that these men died in order that there might be preserved in our borders equal opportunities for all. Ours is the land of the free. Here is government of and by and for the people. We know no rank. Birth brings no title. Before each individual is opened every door, and to him who wills and strives there is no place of influence or power which does not hold out the equal invitation. The doors of this institution are not opened to only the children of a privileged class. From the poorest cabin and the richest home, from the lonesome prairie and the crowded city, from the ranks of the humblest toilers and the counting-houses of the richest merchants, from farm and factory and shop and office you come, and come on equal terms, with equal opportunities before you, and to take in after life not the glory which your fathers give you, but that which you yourselves are able to win. From a humble farmhouse in Ohio, through the gateways of this school, passed a modest, resolute young man, to become the great commander; the present General of the Army commenced life as a mere clerk; and a private soldier is now the President of the United States.

And the end is not yet. That which was so yesterday is so to-day, and will be so to-morrow. The barefoot boy may thank God and take courage, for beneath the Stars and Stripes the future is his. "Whosoever will" not only expresses the assurances of the Gospel, but is also the law of American life and success. It must be remembered, however, that there is a world-wide difference between "whosoever will" and "whosoever simply wishes." The one implies a resolute and unfailing purpose controlling all activities, while the other carries with it nothing but lazy desire. The one is the assurance of success, the other deserves the failure which it receives. Of the thousand men in our land who succeed, luck may be the accident of one, but the other nine hundred and ninety-nine toil for and win it. No one can sit on a dry-goods box and whittle himself into wealth, or stand on the street corner and talk himself into learning, position or power. Before every one is the open door of opportunity; "whosoever will" may enter. And this fact of equal opportunity and equal right has been strengthened and made more far-reaching through the devotion of those whose names are written on this column. They died not in defense of a princely class, not to perpetuate an aristocracy of wealth or birth, but rather to lift a race into the large domain of equal rights and equal opportunities. They heard the sad, pathetic voice of him who walked from the lonesome home of poverty and ignorance through the untiring strength of his own earnestness and ability to the chief magistracy of the nation and a place among the immortals of earth; and, heeding that voice, they died in order that this government of and by and for the people should not perish from the face of the earth, but should continue with a more complete and glorious affirmance of equal rights and equal opportunities for all.

And I want here to say that this doctrine of equal rights and equal opportunities which has always been the theory of our political and social institutions is, notwithstanding some idle talk, still, as ever, the significant fact of our life. The great accumulations of money are not in the hands of those who inherited, but of those who themselves accumulated it; and when I read, as I often do, the denunciations in certain quarters of inordinate wealth, I find almost without an exception that the names connected with that wealth are the names of men who started in life without a dollar. Who are the leaders of our thought to-day? Who are the great men in intellectual life? Who are the inventors and authors, the orators and poets? Who are they that give direction and guidance to the thought and business and high ambition of the nation? Did they come from any class? Were they born into station? Did they come from some privileged rank? On the contrary, as you run over the list of names, you will find that no rank, or class, or place monopolized their beginnings. Their power and influence is something which they themselves have won, and not something which they inherited. The humblest child may look upon the White House with expectation. The poorest and most friendless student may begin with faith and hope his struggle for a seat on the highest bench of the nation. A place in the halls of Congress is not a thing of purchase or inheritance, and the few exceptions which occur only attest the fact as well as the strength and vigor of the rule. This is to-day, and God grant that it may ever remain, a land of equal rights and equal opportunities, not an equality of life and living which is compelled, for wherever there is such compulsion there is slavery, whether the master be a single despot or a mob, but the equality of the Declaration of Independence, the equal possession of "certain unalienable rights . . . life, liberty, and the pursuit of happiness"; the right of each individual to choose for himself his life and work and to pursue that life and work subject to no dominion, and realizing all the success that the intensity of his life and work deserve.

It is fitting that this memorial to the officers and soldiers of the regular army who died in the recent war should be here, for this is the military center of the nation, the great school of those who are to be the officers and commanders; and it is well that the lessons of those patriotic and heroic lives should ever be present before the young who shall come to prepare themselves to take the places they filled and glorified. It was fitting also that this work should have been undertaken and carried through by the surviving officers and soldiers of the army, for it is your comrades' memory that is thus preserved.

Here let this column rise in stately beauty, proclaiming to the coming generations the great occasion and the great truths which have caused it to be. And may every ripple of yonder stream, as it passes and floats onward toward the commercial metropolis of the nation, bear from its lips to the tomb where sleeps the coffined dust of the great commander, the assurances of the unvarying loyalty of the army of the United States now and hereafter to the heroic ideas and ideals of his life, to peace with equal rights and privileges to all.

EPILOGUE.

THIS granite shaft stands not as a memorial alone, but for a principle. It bears witness to the supremacy of discipline and education in the vocation of arms. It vindicates the professional soldier. It glorifies obedience, self-restraint, intelligence. It stands for duty, professional honor, responsibility, order, precision. In the polished integrity of its unbroken mass the primeval granite, upright and unswerving, points heavenward the path of patriotism and of honor.

This is the only monument on the continent to the officers and soldiers of the Regular Army who fought in the War of the Rebellion, and in presenting it to the government of the great republic it has served so well, that army asks its fellow-citizens to bear in remembrance, together with the names of the leaders inscribed upon it — McPherson, Sedgwick, Reynolds, Mansfield, Lyon — those survivors who belong with them to history, officers of the Regular Army and sons also of that Military Academy where their memory is preserved and venerated.

Army Commanders.

Grant	Hooker	Pope
Sherman	Rosecrans	Slocum
Sheridan	McClellan	Canby
Meade	Halleck	Wright, G.
Thomas	Buell	McDowell
Schofield	Ord	Curtis, S. R.
	Howard	

Corps Commanders.

Reynolds, J. F. } 1st.
Newton }

Hancock }
Couch } 2d.
Humphreys }

Heintzelman } 3d.
French }

Keyes }
Gordon Granger } 4th.
Stanley }

Sykes }
Warren } 5th.
Griffin }

Smith, W. F. } 6th.
Wright, H. G. }

Steele } 7th.
Reynolds, J. J. }

Parke, 9th.
Gillmore, 10th.
Williams, 12th.
Davis, J. C., 14th.
Smith, A. J., 16th.
Foster, J. G., 18th.

Franklin }
Emory } 19th.
Grover }

McCook, 20th.
Augur, 22d.
Hartsuff, 23d.
Gibbon, 24th.
Weitzel, 25th.

Stoneman }
Pleasonton }
Merritt } Cavalry.
Wilson, J. H. }

Fitz John Porter, 5th.

Division Commanders.

Doubleday	McCall	Carlin
Stevens	Robinson, J. C.	Morgan, J. D.
Ricketts	Barnes	Hazen
Rufus King	Getty	Ransom
Richardson	Russell, D.	Martindale
Webb	Neill	Palmer
Hays, W.	Seymour	Wessels
Sully	Davidson	Sherman, T.
Hays, A.	Carr	Abercrombie
Berry	Wilcox	Ruger
Prince	Brannan	Kautz
Hamilton	Saxton	Jackson, R. H.
Whipple, A. W.	Ames	Buford
Elliott, W. L.	Turner	Gregg
Wood	Gordon, G. H.	Custer
Casey	Greene, G. H.	Kilpatrick
Ayers	Smith, C. F.	Upton
Morell	Baird	Mackenzie

And their non-graduate brothers-in-arms of the Regular Army.

Corps Commanders.

Sumner	Butterfield
Sickles	Terry

Division Commanders.

Kearny	Harney
Miles	De Trobriand
Mower	

This is the verdict of the greatest war of modern times, given also with equal emphasis in the case of our antagonists — tried in a hundred battles and justified by the results of a score of campaigns. No lesson in war was ever more inevitable, clear-cut and decisive. After a desperate struggle of four years, involving over three millions of combatants, the officers of a little body of ten thousand regulars, almost wholly graduates of the Military Academy at West Point, command as Lieutenant- or Major-Generals every army in the field, nearly all of the Army Corps, and a large proportion of the Divisions.

They head every Supply Corps of the General Staff, and hold every important command in these Corps. They have organized and directed that immense mobilizing and supplying mechanism without which victory would have been impossible, and whose efficiency in the face of enormous difficulties was the wonder and admiration of the military world. They gave to the century two of its greatest commanders, and from their body came the President of the Confederacy and the successor of the immortal Lincoln, all sons of West Point and of the Regular Army.

This sweeping result achieved itself as the gradual but inevitable logic of experience in the face of a political favoritism and demoralization without limit or precedent.

NAMES OF
OFFICERS AND ENLISTED MEN BORNE
UPON
THE BATTLE MONUMENT

OFFICERS.

General Officers.

Brigadier-Generals.

Joseph K. F. Mansfield, Maj.-Gen. Vols., Antietam, Md.
James B. McPherson, Maj.-Gen. Vols., Atlanta, Ga.

General Staff.

Lieut.-Col. Julius P. Garesché, Adjt.-Gen. Dept., Murfreesboro, Tenn.
Surgeon William J. H. White, Medical Dept., Antietam, Md.
Capt. Guilford D. Bailey, Subsistence Dept., Fair Oaks, Va.
Capt. Otis H. Tillinghast, Quartermaster Dept., 1st Bull Run, Va.

Corps of Engineers.

Majors.

Amiel W. Whipple, Maj.-Gen. Vols., Chancellorsville, Va.
James St. C. Morton, Petersburg, Va.

Captains.

Holdimand S. Putnam, Fort Wagner, S. C.
Charles E. Cross, Rappahannock River, Va.
Arthur H. Dutton, Bermuda Hundred, Va.

First Lieutenants.
Patrick H. O'Rorke, Col. Vols., Gettysburg, Pa.
John R. Meigs, Harrisonburg, Va.

Corps of Topographical Engineers.
First Lieutenants.
J. L. Kirby Smith, Corinth, Miss.
Orlando G. Wagner, Yorktown, Va.

Ordnance Department.
Captains.
Jesse L. Reno, Maj.-Gen. Vols., South Mountain, Md.
George C. Strong, Brig.-Gen. Vols., Fort Wagner, S. C.

1st Cavalry.
Captains.
Benjamin F. Davis, Beverly Ford, Va.
Samuel McKee, Cold Harbor, Va.

First Lieutenants.
Robert Allen, Jr., Gaines's Mill, Va.
Cæsar R. Fisher, Ashby's Gap, Va.
Frederick C. Ogden, Trevillian Station, Va.
Joseph S. Hoyer, Smithfield, Va.
John H. Nichols, Trevillian Station, Va.
John S. Walker, Harper's Ferry, Va.

2d Cavalry.
Captains.
Charles W. Canfield, Beverly Ford, Va.
James F. McQuesten, Opequan, Va.

First Lieutenants.
Michael Lawless, Trevillian Station, Va.
Charles McMaster, Front Royal, Va.

Second Lieutenant.
George DeV. Selden, Gettysburg, Pa.

3d Cavalry.
Captain.
Alexander McRae, Valverde, N. M.

Second Lieutenant.
George Harrington, Memphis, Tenn.

4th Cavalry.
Colonel.
John Sedgwick, Maj.-Gen. Vols., Spottsylvania C. H., Va.

Captain.
George D. Bayard, Brig.-Gen. Vols., Fredericksburg, Va.

First Lieutenant.
Elbridge G. Roys, Selina, Ala.

Second Lieutenants.
Thomas Healy, Franklin, Tenn.
Francis C. Wood, Middleton, Tenn.

5th Cavalry.
Captains.
Thomas Drummond, Five Forks, Va.
Joseph P. Ash, Todd's Tavern, Va.
James Cahill, Todd's Tavern, Va.

First Lieutenants.

John J. Sweet, Gaines's Mill, Va.
Richard Byrnes, Lieut.-Col. Vols., Cold Harbor, Va.
Joseph P. Henley, Trevillian Station, Va.
Richard Fitzgerald, Winchester, Va.
John Trevor, Winchester, Va.

6th Cavalry.

Captains.

William P. Sanders, Brig.-Gen. Vols., Knoxville, Tenn.
Charles R. Lowell, Brig.-Gen. Vols., Middletown, Va.

First Lieutenants.

Peter McGrath, Apache Canon, N. M.
Isaac M. Ward, Beverly Ford, Va.
Christian Balder, Gettysburg, Pa.
Thomas W. Simson, wounds received in battle.
Andrew Stoll, Beverly Ford, Va.

Second Lieutenant.

Hugh McQuade, Bull Run, Va.

1st Artillery.

Captain.

Lewis O. Morris, Col. Vols., Cold Harbor, Va.

First Lieutenants.

Douglas Ramsay, 1st Bull Run, Va.
Edward B. Hill, White Oak Swamp, Va.
Justin E. Dimick, Chancellorsville, Va.
Edmund Kirby, Brig.-Gen. Vols., Chancellorsville, Va.
George A. Woodruff, Gettysburg, Pa.
Philip D. Mason, Trevillian Station, Va.

Second Lieutenant.
James A. Sanderson, Pleasant Hill, La.

2d Artillery.

Captain.
Henry Benson, Malvern Hill, Va.

First Lieutenant.
John T. Greble, Big Bethel, Va.

Second Lieutenants.
Presley O. Craig, 1st Bull Run, Va.
Thomas Burnes, Hatcher's Run, Va.
Samuel D. Southworth, Cedar Creek, Va.

3d Artillery.

Second Lieutenants.
William D'Wolf, Williamsburg, Va.
Manning Livingston, Gettysburg, Pa.
Robert Floyd, Chickamauga, Ga.

4th Artillery.

Captain.
George W. Hazzard, White Oak Swamp, Va.

First Lieutenants.
William L. Baker, Antietam, Md.
George Dickinson, Fredericksburg, Va.
Franklin B. Crosby, Chancellorsville, Va.
Bayard Wilkeson, Gettysburg, Pa.
Alonzo H. Cushing, Gettysburg, Pa.

5th Artillery.

Major.

Thomas Williams, **Brig.-Gen. Vols.**, Baton Rouge, La.

Captains.

William R. Terrill, **Brig.-Gen. Vols.**, Perryville, Ky.
John R. Smead, 2d **Bull Run**, Va.
Henry V. De Hart, Gaines's Mill, Va.
Stephen H. Weed, **Brig.-Gen. Vols.**, Gettysburg, Pa.

First Lieutenants.

Henry W. Kingsbury, Antietam, Md.
Charles E. Hazlett, Gettysburg, Pa.
Howard M. Burnham, Chickamauga, Ga.

Second Lieutenants.

William W. Williams, Boonsboro, Md.
Henry M. Baldwin, Cedar Creek, Va.

1st Infantry.

Capt. James E. Powell, Shiloh, Tenn.
Second Lieut. Charles Wilkins, Vicksburg, Miss.

2d Infantry.

Colonel.

Dixon S. Miles, Harper's Ferry, Va.

Captains.

Nathaniel Lyon, **Brig.-Gen. Vols.**, Wilson's Creek, Mo.
Salem S. Marsh, Chancellorsville, Va.
Richard Brindley, Gaines's Mill, Va.
Samuel A. McKee, Greenwich, Va.

First Lieutenants.
Frank C. Goodrich, Gettysburg, Pa.
Ralph E. Ellinwood, 2d Bull Run, Va.

Second Lieutenants.
Thomas D. Parker, Gaines's Mill, Va.
William Kidd, 2d Bull Run, Va.

3d Infantry.

Major.
Nathan B. Russell, Gaines's Mill, Va.

First Lieutenant.
Woods McGuire, Malvern Hill, Va.

4th Infantry.

Major.
Seneca G. Simmons, Glendale, Va.

Captains.
Julius W. Adams, Gaines's Mill, Va.
Charles H. Brightly, Wilderness, Va.

First Lieutenant.
Ira F. Gensel, Fredericksburg, Va.

5th Infantry.

Colonel.
John F. Reynolds, Maj.-Gen. Vols., Gettysburg, Pa.

Captain.
Benjamin Wingate, Valverde, N. M.

First Lieutenant.
Lyman Mishler, Valverde, N. M.

6th Infantry.
Colonel.
Edward A. King, Chickamauga, Ga.

Captain.
Rennselaer W. Foote, Gaines's Mill, Va.

7th Infantry.
Captain.
George Ryan, Laurel Hill, Va.

First Lieutenants.
Wesley F. Miller, Gettysburg, Pa.
Richard R. Crawford, Gettysburg, Pa.
Frederick E. Crossman, Weldon Railroad, Va.

8th Infantry.
Majors.
Joseph B. Plummer, Brig.-Gen. Vols., Wilson's Creek, Mo.
David A. Russell, Brig.-Gen. Vols., Opequan, Va.

First Lieutenant.
Otis Fisher, Poplar Spring Church, Va.

10th Infantry.
Captains.
Jesse A. Gove, Col. Vols., Chickahominy, Va.
William G. Jones, Col. Vols., Chickamauga, Ga.

First Lieutenants.
William J. Fisher, Gettysburg, Pa.
Richard Skinner, Petersburg, Va.

Second Lieutenants.
Michael C. Boyce, Gettysburg, Pa.
James Henry, Wilderness, Va.

11th Infantry.

Captain.
Thomas O. Barri, Gettysburg, Pa.

First Lieutenants.
Herbert Kenaston, Gettysburg, Pa.
Matthew Elder, Gettysburg, Pa.
Wright Staples, Wilderness, Va.
Charles I. Pleasants, Wilderness, Va.
James P. Pratt, Bethesda Church, Va.

Second Lieutenants.
Henry Rochford, Gettysburg, Pa.
Amaziah J. Barber, Gettysburg, Pa.

12th Infantry.

Major.
Luther B. Bruen, Laurel Hill, Va.

Captains.
John G. Read, 2d Bull Run, Va.
Thomas M. Hulings, Spottsylvania Court House, Va.
Samuel S. Newbury, Weldon Railroad, Va.
Frederick Winthrop, Bvt. Brig.-Gen. Vols., Five Forks, Va.
William Sergeant, Gravelly Run, Va.

First Lieutenants.

Jean P. Wagner, Wilderness, Va.
August Eggemeyer, Bethesda Church, Va.
Thomas D. Urmston, Chapel House, Va.

Second Lieutenants.

Charles F. Van Duzer, Gaines's Mill, Va.
Silas A. Miller, Gettysburg, Pa.

13th Infantry.

Captains.

Edward C. Washington, Vicksburg, Miss.
Archibald H. Engle, Resaca, Ga.
Cornelius W. Tolles, Newton, Va.

First Lieutenant.

Justus A. Boies, Vicksburg, Miss.

14th Infantry.

Captains.

Patrick E. Burke, Col. Vols., Rome Cross Roads, Ga.
Roderic Stone, Valverde, N. M.
Sullivan W. Burbank, Wilderness, Va.
Hamlin W. Keyes, Spottsylvania Court House, Va.
James F. McElhone, Bvt. Lieut.-Col., Gaines's Mill, Va.

First Lieutenants.

Warren W. Chamberlain, 2d Bull Run, Va.
Daniel M. Broadhead, Wilderness, Va.

Second Lieutenants.

George W. Hoover, Gaines's Mill, Va.
John K. Clay, Spottsylvania Court House, Va.
Thomas E. Collins, Wilderness, Va.

15th Infantry.

Captains.

William W. Wise, Stone River, Tenn.
Jacob B. Bell, Stone River, Tenn.
Charles G. Harker, Kenesaw Mountain, Ga.

Second Lieutenant.

Joseph C. Forbes, New Hope Church, Ga.

16th Infantry.

Major.

Sidney Coolidge, Chickamauga, Ga.

Captains.

William H. Acker, Shiloh, Tenn.
George N. Bascom, Valverde, N. M.
Patrick T. Keyes, Shiloh, Tenn.
Alexander Hays, Brig.-Gen. Vols., Wilderness, Va.
Patrick Kelly, Col. Vols., Petersburg, Va.

First-Lieutenants.

Edward L. Mitchell, Shiloh, Tenn.
Homer H. Clark, Chickamauga, Ga.

Second Lieutenant.

Peter J. Coenzler, Mission Ridge, Tenn.

17th Infantry.

Captains.

Albert Dodd, Gaines's Mill, Va.
Henry J. McLandburgh, Fredericksburg, Va.
William J. Temple, Chancellorsville, Va.
Alexander Wilkin, Col. Vols., Tupelo, Miss.

First Lieutenants.

Charles T. Weld, Chancellorsville, Va.
William H. Chamberlin, Gettysburg, Pa.
Edward S. Abbot, Gettysburg, Pa.
Frank E. Stimpson, Laurel Hill, Va.
John T. Dowling, Laurel Hill, Va.

18th Infantry.

Captains.

Charles E. Denison, Murfreesboro, Tenn.
Charles L. Kneass, Murfreesboro, Tenn.
John A. Thompson, Hoover's Gap, Tenn.

First Lieutenants.

James Simons, Murfreesboro, Tenn.
Joseph McConnell, Murfreesboro, Tenn.
Charles L. Truman, Chickamauga, Ga.
Lucius F. Brown, Chickamauga, Ga.

Second Lieutenants.

John F. Hitchcock, Murfreesboro, Tenn.
John Lane, Chickamauga, Ga.

19th Infantry.

Majors.

Stephen D. Carpenter, Murfreesboro, Tenn.
George L. Willard, Col. Vols., Gettysburg, Pa.

First Lieutenant.

Michael B. Fogarty, Chickamauga, Ga.

Second Lieutenant.

Charles F. Miller, Chickamauga, Ga.

ENLISTED MEN.

Battalion of Engineers.
Private Thomas Berry
Martin C. Kehoe

Ordnance Corps.
Carriage-maker Henry Thesang

Signal Corps.
Sergeant John Corrigan
Private Philip W. Ashton
Amos P. Barnes
Abraham E. Borden
Andrew P. Cobb
Alexander McCollim

General Service.
Private Thomas Ronon

1st U. S. Cavalry.
First Sergeant Henry Montraville
Frederick Papp
Sergeant Jasper R. Boyles

Thomas J. Clark
Edwin Chutland
James Kelly
Adolph Meyer
Thomas Montgomery
William Mulcahy
Charles Oertel
James Rathburn
James A. Samo
Corporal Henry C. Albert
William T. Bennett
Samuel A. Carr
William H. Cole
George A. Cullison
John Hall
James T. Holt
Peter Latti
Thomas Leary
John Mallen
Michael Mulcahy
Jacob McAtee
James O'Connor
Charles A. Tankersly
Charles Pfil
Lucius F. Walden
Adam Ziegler
Blacksmith Timothy Muldowny
Farrier Andrew Van Camp
Bugler William H. Burritt
Musician Frank Dawson
Private Hubbard Babcock
John Beacon
Samuel Bell
William Blumhardt

AT WEST POINT

John B. Brown
Elijah Comstock
Jacob Deeds
Mark Dolby
August Echolett
Henry S. Fetrow
William Gallop
John A. Gibbons
Joseph Hagin
George Hannon
Warren F. Hedges
Frederick Hensinger
Charles Hoffman
Nelson Johnson
James Kearney
William Kellier
Lewis Ladue
John J. Livingston
Daniel Lynch
Martin V. Mathewson
John McCafferty
James McHugh
Hugh Meegan
Henry Miller
William J. Mincen
William Monroe
John Normoyle
John A. O'Carroll
George Ott
William Peter
John Radeford
Charles Reinstein
James Rodgers
William Scott

John Smith
John M. Smith
Samuel Stinebarger
Jacob Steinhauser
John R. Sulivan
Thomas Thews
Peter Welgong
John F. Zeitler

2d U. S. Cavalry.

First Sergeant Ephriam Adams
Henry Kinzler
Sergeant Martin Bailey
James Carr
John D. Dunbar
Christian Fisher
James Hanna
Andrew Moore
Charles Vanmeter
Corporal John C. Annis
John Buckhardt
Stephen Hogan
William H. Keiger
Truman King
Patrick Morglu
Luke Ollis
Albert Roe
Edward Shuhey
Peter B. Worden
Martin Zimmer
Saddler David C. Dinim
Wilhelm Oleker
Bugler John Robinson
Private Richard F. Ambrose

Joseph Anderson
John Barrington
John Blael
Emil Briede
Ariel C. Chapin
Thomas Clark
John Conover
Samuel A. Cook
William Cooper
Thomas Corbeth
Andrew B. Couch
James Courtney
Daniel Crimmins
James Dean
Daniel Denison
John Driscoll
Joseph Eckels
Rudolph Engel
James Ferris
Philip Fitzsimons
Charles Frick
Michael Gahe
Edward Gorman
Harvey D. **Haynes**
Leo Henze
Frederic Hood
George Hozzell
Frederick Kauffman
William Kline
Patrick McArdle
John McCullough
Thomas McTague
Rodney A. Manning
Andrew L. Metts

Michael Mooney
Patrick Murray
Michael O'Brien
John Philips
Thomas N. Prentice
James Levens
Patrick Rhatigan
James Ruseher
Charles Smith
Samuel E. Smith
John T. Thompson
James Tryon
Charles W. Uber
Charles Williams

3d U. S. Cavalry.

Sergeant Thomas M. Brierley
John J. Knox
Francis O'Cain
Corporal James E. Brophey
Thomas Hughes
Bugler Albert Shott
Musician Henry Ebert
Private Peter Beatty
Theodore Braun
Edward Carey
William J. Dake
Edward Doyle
John Finn
Bartley Folan
James Hughes
John Lane
John Ludwig
James McDougal

Patrick Scanlon
Thomas Sharda
Eli W. Smith
Samuel Smith
Erley P. Turman
William E. Wade
John Weckesser
John H. Westervelt

4th U. S. Cavalry.
Sergeant John Carmichael
Martin Murphy
John Rankin
Joseph B. Richmond
James Walsh
Corporal Martin Birmingham
Patrick Cuddehy
Phelix Cullan
Frederick Hall
Frederick W. Klein
George Phillips
Stephen Wetzberger
Farrier Alexander Millright
2d Class Musician Frederick Shafer
Alfred S. Toy
Private Frank Bars
John Baum
Bartholomew Burke
George Cassell
Commodore P. Cole
Charles Cowarden
Patrick Craven
David Daugherty
Robert P. Doyle

138   THE BATTLE MONUMENT

John Entwhistle
Napoleon M. King
Andrew J. Mahoney
Daniel McDonell
James Orange
Archibald B. Orr
John Parsons
Levi L. Pettitt
Friend Pratt
Henry J. Preas
Fretrick Rhyman
Philip H. Saller
William Sawyer
Adolph Stettler
Rodger Stokes
Patrick Tracy
Nathan Writhe
Colored Cook Jackson Kelley

5th U. S. Cavalry.
Sergeant Thomas Barrett
John Doherty
Franklin S. Ginginer
Henry Hedrick
Corporal Charles E. Asher
David Courtney
George T. Crawford
Aquilla Hart
Michael Howard
James H. Oliver
Lewis J. Robage
Musician Christopher Buermann
Bugler Edward Feldhiene
Private Ira K. Bailey

Benni D. Bailey
John Bigmone
Clarence O. Bingen
John C. Burk
George Burrhus
Michael Canton
Walter R. Covington
Francis Croal
John Curran
Edward Dolan
Domian Erne
Patrick Galliger
Peter Gillasper
Samuel Gindrat
Francis Hogan
William Johns
Patrick Kenny
William H. King
William Larison
James Lason
William H. Lazier
Gustaf Lindell
Thomas Miller
Preston O. Morse
Charles Olens
Alexander Rayner
David F. Roberts
Barney Ryan
Charles W. Sanders
Jacob Schneider
John Schlotterer
George Segerer
John Siepe
Vinton T. Swallow

William Talday
Edmond Whelan
William W. Wright
Recruit Jacob Schlichter

6th U. S. Cavalry.

Sergeant William Ellsworth
Miles L. Ten Eyck
James McCallister
John Pattinson
Frank Schweigus
Corporal William Alexander
Alonzo Ellsworth
John H. Erb
John Manice
David C. Oby
Saddler Robert McElroy
Bugler Edson S. Cooke
Private George D. Bartlett
George Beckert
Henry Borden
William A. Boyntion
Charles Croissant
Patrick Doyle
Henry Eisle
James Evans
Edward Falkner
John Fisher
James W. Gillispie
Lyman W. Hale
Joshua Heakin
Christian F. Hildenbrand
Abel A. Irish
James King

AT WEST POINT

Conrad Klein
Thomas Lee
William D. Masters
William L. Mattern
Lue Merkle
Francis M. Miller
Lewis Negler
Charles O'Harra
Nathaniel B. Owen
Thomas J. Peterman
Jacob Poet
Nelson Remmington
William R. Reynolds
David A. Thaburn
William H. Thomas
William Vandevender
Joseph F. Vanzant
Spencer Viall
Samuel Wilson

1st U. S. Artillery.

Sergeant Alfred J. Carber
Thomas Kirnan
Edward F. McNamara
Henry Rukert
Corporal William Ferguson
John W. Mahany
Musician John S. Blaney
Private James Allen
James Allum
Christian A. Andler
Charles Baker
Michael Barrey
William Bates

Edward Beavin
Henry Bergmann
John Buckley
Patrick Broderick
James Campbell
Rowland Card
John Casey
Daniel B. Chase
Philip Clarke
Daniel B. Cofrin
John Connellan
Charles Cooley
Daniel Curly
Michael Dillon
John Donoghue
Richard Forsyth
Edward Gallwey
Jacob Gilb
James Gilmore
John Gray
Arsenal H. Griffin
Edward Grove
Martin **Halloran**
Rollin E. **Hartwell**
Andrew Hauss
Horace Holmes
John Hopkins
Daniel Hough
Frank E. Houghton
John Irvin
Patrick Kerrigan
James Killion
John King
Abraham LaFayette

James Little
Samuel J. Lewis
John J. Mackey
John Marklein
Henry Miles
Patrick McGuinity
James R. Mooney
Andrew McLeer
George A. Nutter
Shalto O'Brien
Thomas Padgett
Joseph H. Parslow
Henry Platt
Frederick Renard
Charles Rivers
John Roache
George Royce
Robert Rummler
John Shafer
John Shea
William H. Smith
August Stein
John Stoltz
Peter Struthers
James B. Terney
James F. Wheeler
William H. Whitehouse
John C. Wood
William S. Worcester

2d U. S. Artillery.
First Sergeant William Scott
Sergeant Samuel Bollinger
Herman O. Gotz

Corporal George D. Cook
Josiah Steele
Private Franklin F. Allen
Charles Ammerman
William Baird
Garrett Barry
Henry Beck
John Bergamin
Adolphus Bhoy
John Campbell
William Cope
Martin Corbet
Hugh Donaghue
William Finley
Henry Foster
Vandy Franklin
Martin Gilroy
William H. Grover
William Guth
Randolph Hand
George Hang
Arthur Hardes
John Hitz
Henry Horstman
Jacob Huber
William Lacumber
Patrick Loughery
Joseph Margery
Charles Mathers
Emmore Moore
Michael S. Moriarty
John E. Mowrer
Timothy McSweeny
John B. Norris

AT WEST POINT

Silvester Parker
Richard Powers
John Prisen
Philip Reehil
Charles Ritchie
George W. Ritchmond
John W. Semline
Daniel Spane
John W. Them
Augustus Van Dwingle
Oliver Wren

3d U. S. Artillery.
Sergeant Robert Ames
Bugler John W. Sarguson
Private Jacob Altheer
Ackerman Anderson
Mathew Ashton
Alfred Barnard
Benjamin Bayliss
George C. Bentley
Henry Boothbey
William Brown
Charles W. Carlton
Denis Carroll
John Clifford
Michael Conroy
Andrew Cooley
James George
Amos Y. Harry
Arthur Hughes
William H. Hurlbut
Francis M. Hutchings
Charles A. Kratka

James King
Bernard Laughran
John Malone
Dennis Murphy
John McIntyre
Sylvester Nordike
Charles H. Pinkham
Henry Reinschoss
Rudolph Richner
James Rice
James H. Riddel
Henry Schaffer
Jeremiah Shehan
Charles H. Taylor
Augustus Tainter
Perry S. White
Michael Woods
William Wright

4th U. S. Artillery.

Sergeant Samuel L. Buell
Charles Ellis
Andrew Fay
Joseph Herzog
Corporal Frederick Bright
Theodore L. Williamson
Artificer Dennis Maloney
Bugler David R. Patrick
Private Benjamin Anderson
William Anderson
Christian Aungst
Richard Bannin
John Brown
John Burns

Jeremiah Butler
Joseph A. Campbell
Reuben A. Cary
Cosmas M. Cecil
Jacob Defren
Bartholomew Dempsey
Edward E. Doran
Andrew Dougherty
Edward Dunne
Bryan Charles Eagar
John Edgecombe
Henry Elmer
William E. Emory
Francis Enright
Ansel Fassett
Adolph Freitag
Franz A. Fugmann
Henry Geary
Shelby Gray
John Grennin
Dwight F. Griswold
George Haffner
George W. Hall
John Hickey
Charles F. Hoefer
Patrick Hogan
Samuel C. Hooker
William M. Howard
William Kavanagh
Bartly Kelly
Peter Kelly
Ellis A. Kingsbury
Timothy Larry
Andrew J. Lowe

Henry P. Lyons
John Marley
John Mayberry
William McNeal
David A. Meneilly
Andrew F. Missimer
James Murphy
Lewis Murphy
Patrick O'Connor
Willis H. Patrick
William Patton
Ervin L. Pepper
Samuel Powell
Luke Roach
Reuben Rowley
Gustavus Sachse
Patrick Savage
Martin Scanlon
Paul Schur
Frank Scudder
Peter Schutzle
John Sheahan
Franz Smith
Henry Strait
James Thompson
William Travillion
Norbare B. Walcott
Thomas Wallace
Edward H. Ward
Edward D. West
William H. Williams
George W. **Yapp**

AT WEST POINT

5th U. S. Artillery.

Sergeant David Cain Bickel
Frederick O'Donnell
James Scanlon
Corporal John Philip Edwin Brader
John Coushmaghnan
Thomas Davison
Martin Dooley
Michael Graham
George W. Houk
William Kirkwood
Michael McGrath
Charles V. Osborn
Artificer Jonathan Robeson
Private Alexander Allen
John Allen
John Andrews
Eugene Brower
Charles Burger
James Carrell
Robert Chamberlin
Thomas Cleary
John B. Cochran
John Collins
Joseph Cooper
John Costello
James Cullen
Frederick Deasonbach
Bernard Des Gouttes
Michael Driscoll
John Duffy
Christian Enzlan
Charles Geiger
Jacob Gobriel

Thomas Green
Lewis C. Griswold
Henry Harris
Francis Harrison
George Helshaw
Jesaias M. Heydt
Martin Higgins
James Hoobler
David T. Howard
Henry Jersey
Adonija Jewell.
Dennis Kennedy
Samuel W. Lafferty
Thomas Maloney
James Mathews
Robert Morrison
Francis Mourey
James F. McAulis
Martin McFadden
James McGlindon
John McMahon
John Munhall
William Naylor
Peter Nugent
James O'Brien
Michael O'Donnell
Henry Owens
Frank Packard
Ashford Painter
Benjamin Putt
Frederick A. Reig
Henry Ripley
Samuel Rodenberger
Louis Row

Thomas C. Stone
Peter Sharrow
George Shafer
John Searfoss
Daniel E. Sickles
Jacob J. Snyder
Edwin H. Taylor
Leander Taylor
James Turner
Joseph W. Tuttle
Andrew Wagner
Denis Walles
John Walsh
Thomas Worts

1st U. S. Infantry.

Sergeant Joseph T. Nichols
Willis B. Worth
Corporal George I. Doller
Henry Harbold
Private Jacob Baehr
Adam Brangle
Edward Brawn
Patrick Daniel
James Doig
Samuel Furter
Sylvester Johnson
John Johnston
John Kerns
Ferdinand Knaut
August Kruger
William Lazarus
George W. Lee
John Long

John Lynch
Daniel Murray
William McGann
Joseph A. McMullan
Timothy Neligan
Edward O'Donnell
William Peacock
James Pinkerton
John Res
William F. Rock
Napoleon Sherzinger
Jacob Stahlman
Adam Sturmfels

2d U. S. Infantry.
First Sergeant Rudolph Thieme
Sergeant Thomas S. Camp
Werner Jahres
Thomas Madigan
Rudolph Zimmerman
Corporal George Butler
William H. Butler
William Carney
Ezra C. French
John Fullbright
James Kelly
Frederick Kousenmiller
Patrick Rourke
Musician Theodore A. Miller
Private William Bankhouse
William L. Barnes
Lawrence Belfour
Michael Bogan
William J. Bond

John Bradly
Robert Brown
George W. Bush
Terence Carroll
Francis R. Chesbro
Charles C. Cleaver
John Cooly
John Cooper
Thomas Cosgrove
Thomas E. Donnellan
Michael Donnelly
James Eugene
George D. Fenner
William Fitch
Michael Gonzel
Adam Groh
John Hare
Useb Harper
Louis Hartman
Michael Heath
Charles A. Hedges
William Heuratty
Peter Hickey
Walter Hill
William Hunter
William Johnson
Peter Kelly
James Kenny
John Kenney
Leslie Laporte
William Loyd
James Mackle
John Magarry
William Malony

David Martin
James Meehan
August Meyer
Nicholas McDonough
Stephen McGinnity
Peter McNulty
Augustus Mier
James McGinn
William H. Nixon
Christian Orb
Maurice Pepper
George Reynolds
Lucus Rittler
James E. Rugers
Austin Sadler
John Selinon
James Sheehan
Joseph Shupfer
Godfrey Smith
Henry Smith
Augustus Stahl
Joseph Theiring
James Trainer
Frank Uhrman
N. D. Van Ormun
Francis Vanston
Michael Walsh
Patrick Welch
John Wells
John Weston
Richard White
John Willis
Patrick Woods
Homer Young

AT WEST POINT

3d U. S. Infantry.

First Sergeant Francis P. Litzinger
Corporal Charles H. Canwell
Harry Loraine
Malcolm J. Montford
John Toner
Private Nicholas Applebury
James Beaty
Gilbert H. Beverly
Peter Bingel
John Brennan
James County
Thomas Dalton
David Dreakes
Robert Furlong
John A. Gale
Michael Groustine
Robert Haley
William S. Holmes
Frederick Jansen
Benjamin F. Kellog
Thomas Kennedy
Maurice Knopfmacher
Caspard Kupferk
Mathew Lodin
Charles F. Long
John Murrey
Patrick McDonald
John McManamin
John Pyne
Philip Rodel
Luke Shaughnessy
Michael J. Smith
Patrick Sullivan

Peter Sullivan
Patrick Tighe
Mark White
Edward M. Williams

4th U. S. Infantry.
Sergeant Timb Doherty
John Flynn
Louis Planmann
John Riely
John J. Strain
Corporal Michael McGarvey
William O'Brien
German Restell
James Rogerson
Private Christian Albert
Ernest A. C. Aschemoor
William Bonner
Bernard Brady
Randall H. Brunning
Charles Caldwell
James M. Carroll
Michael Carroll
Frederick Case
Richard Casey
John Christensen
Uriah W. Clark
Thomas Conlin
Bernhard Douch
Christian Engers
Charles T. Fox
Henry Grazier
William Hamilton
William Harnett

William G. Harper
John Kahear
George Lemaine
Patrick Masterson
Bernard McCue
James McDonald
Roger McDonald
Daniel L. McGinn
Peter McManaman
David Meredith
David Miller
Michael McCue
Michael McGuire
James O'Dowd
Gottlieb Ott
John Patterson
Thomas Peters
Isaac Rice
John Rourke
Bennet Robinson
Edward Simpson
Warner R. Thompson
Andreas Waker

5th U. S. Infantry.
First Sergeant Luther Sheppard
Sergeant John Stewart
Corporal Simon Rothschild
Henry Schlutter
Private John Ford
Nicholas Hayes
Joseph Hudson
Patrick Hughes
Andres Kinnberger

Thomas Leary
Jacob Levy
John Murphy
John Pollock
Francis Richard
John Sands
George A. Smith

6th U. S. Infantry.
First Sergeant Julius Thetard
Sergeant Patrick Weare
Corporal Owen Leonard
James L. Lovett
Herman Westhus
Private Thomas Ainsworth
William Brown
James Campbell
Cornelius Collins
James Contoit
John Cook
Charles Costello
John Donoghue
James Dunlap
William Fenton
Frederick H. Hicks
Thomas Jackson
Patrick Kiernan
Barney Lafferty
Cornelius Leo
John Mahony
Patrick Mullen
Charles F. Niemetz
Patrick O'Keeffe
Joseph L. Pinkham

William L. Rutherford
Ransom B. Russell
Christian F. Schmidtzer
Henry Schultz
John Sullivan
John Wilson

7th U. S. Infantry.
Sergeant William James
James M. Rockwell
Timothy Sullivan
Corporal Gustavus Percy
John P. Rumbel
Private Thomas Arnold
John C. Ashton
John A. Bishop
Thomas Carey
John C. Connolly
William H. Curtis
John Douglas
John Ellard
John Fitzgerald
Joseph Folgen
Charles Forrest
Julius Furgeson
Eugene F. Gibbins
Michael Gill
Thomas Gilling
Alexander Gillon
John H. Jack
Cyrus Junkins
Emile M. Kahn
John Keenan
Peter Keim

Thomas Lawlare
Harvey Lary
John Liebrich
Joseph C. Labadie
William A. Mason
John Mee
William Muller
Bernard McBride
Peter McCue
James McDonald
James Nolan
Edward Nugent
James O'Briene
James Reilly
Pixlee Sherwood
George Smith
Patrick Smith
Philip Shoemaker
John Teahan
William Wilson
Frederick Winscher

8th U. S. Infantry.

Private James Adams
William Bailey
James Cunningham
Robert Boyle
George O. Curtis
William Dougharty
William **Gurl**
John Hanley
Michael Hoag
John Latimer
Martin Molarcky

AT WEST POINT

Christian W. Shafer
William Waldov

9th U. S. Infantry.
(None)

10th U. S. Infantry.
First Sergeant James Carroll
William K. Davis
John Kelly
Sergeant Daniel C. Ballard
Herman Buiter
Thomas Corcoran
Michael Finnaughty
Able Johnston
Corporal James Craig
John A. Crotty
Thomas H. Crotty
Charles Fischer
George W. Green
Robert Hayes
Charles Smith
Low D. Webb
Private Rudolph Arndt
John Battersbee
Francis Blake
Thomas Brady
John C. **Brown**
Patrick Burke
Darby Burns
Hazimier Canomski
Carl Christianson
Francis M. Cleary
Peter Collins

Michael Crogan
Albert J. Cross
Wesley Dailey
James Daley
John E. Davis
Frank Depoire
Edwin Eeney
Michael Feeney
Thomas Fitzpatrick
Richard Gregg
George Harris
Matthew Harrison
Henry Heine
John Henderson
George W. Hicks
John Hoggan
John Igo
Hugh Jeffery
Stephen Jennings
Israel L. Jones
Mathew Kelly
Thomas Kelly
Michael Kennedy
Joseph Kremer
Owen Mahoney
Andrew Marshal
James Marx
George Meins
Frederick Miller
Samuel Miller
John B. Montgomery
Owen McGorman
Patrick McDonell
Peter McKenny

Frank Nelson
Michael Neville
John Noonan
Joseph Odgers
Michael O'Keefe
John C. Orwig
John Parker
Eail Payne
John Reichling
Jacob Rife
Emil Rotwitt
Henry Ruhr
William Schweer
Henry Schwep
John Wesley Smith
John D. Steel
Oliver P. Stewart
Edward Walsh
Charles W. Washburn
Recruit William H. Potter

11th U. S. Infantry.
First Sergeant Thomas O'Connor
John Remsen
Sergeant John P. Birmingham
Edward Britt, Jr.
Frank W. Clock
Alfred E. Cook
William C. Fitzgerald
Patrick Fitzmorris
Henry Clay Ford
Francis Fuchs
James Henry
William H. Heys

Samuel Murphy
H. M. Reed
William H. Thomas
Corporal James B. F. Adams
Josiah S. Estabrook
James M. Fleming
Pulaski Jerome
Ephraim Sands
William P. Woodworth
William Wylie
Private Albert Anderson
Albert Ankerson
George A. Annis
Robert R. Armstrong
John L. Arnold
Joseph Bissonnette
Michael H. Bock
Charles W. Bodman
George J. Brown
Henry Brown
Michael Carew
James D. Cavenagh
John Clahane
John Conway
Philip Corrigan
John Creardon
Michael Curley
Mark Dempsey
Napoleon Dubue
Elias A. Dunkelberg
Albert P. Eagle
Alfred Esset
George W. Fales
Patrick Fallon

James Farrell
Michael Fitzgibbon
John Flangherty
Jeremiah Ford
Louis Fuchs
Benjamin F. Garland
Gedeon Germain
John Goff
John Hanna
Solomon Hannant
Charles Horton
George Jacobs
Otho Jenkins
Darwin Johnson
James Kelley
John Keenan
Jonas Keim
Thomas Kennedy
Thomas W. Laurence
George LaMountain
Henry Lasinger
Henry L. Leighton
Timothy Lowry
Thomas Mallon
Albert Mattice
William Mears
Gottlieb Metsger
John Miller
James F. Mitchell
Patrick Molloy
James Moonay
Casimire Morain
John T. Myers
John McCluskey

Alcott D. McKeen
Charles McElroy
Private John O'Keefe
Richard Parsons
Andrew W. Perkins
John H. Ransom
Henry Reals
William Rising
John Roach
Stapylton Robinson
George Ryan
Thomas F. Ryan
George Scott
Andreas Selyelie
Frank Sheldon
James L. Sholes
George J. Simpson
William I. Sloan
Oliver J. Stork
Levi Strickland
Hubert Stone
William Sullivan
William H. Sullivan
James Sweeney
Henry Thron
Charles H. Tinker
Willard Twichell
George Vanbuskirk
William Walace
Charles Watkins
Virgil I. Wheeler
Luke White
David Wright
Amos B. Wilcox
Charles Wilson

AT WEST POINT

12th U. S. Infantry.

First Sergeant Richard Blakely
Kasper Dusmann
Thomas Earley
Sergeant Peter Black
William A. Eichelberger
Charles Meeks
Joseph Morrison
Valentine B. Oaks
Hugh Rogers
Michael Shannahan
Corporal Ithamer Barbur
William H. Brundage
Charles E. Dunn
Morgan Flanders
John B. McLaughlin
James M. Nelson
William Over
Francis Tracey
Samuel J. Walton
George M. Wark
Joel White
Ludwig Wittstock
Private George Abender
James Aiken
Charles Andrus
William Armstrong
Joseph Ashborne
Patrick Ayres
William D. Baldwin
Anthony Barrett
Solomon Bell
John Biggs
Benjamin F. Black
Justin S. Booth

Anthony Bush
Ezra Carter
James Cassidy
Joseph Champlain
John Chard
Aurora S. Chatfield
John Clark
Patrick Crawford
George Comstock
John Currie
Jacob P. Cutright
James T. Davis
Michael Donavan
Hiram Dunning
William Dushon
Levi Eells
Solomon Eldridge
Patrick Gartland
Eugene Gerard
Philip Glessner
John Gray
Samuel Green
Edward M. Hammond
William Hannegan
George M. Harrington
John Higgins
Charles Hinniker
William H. Hoffman
Samuel Hyland
Martin **James**
Jacob Johnson
Reuben Kelley
Daniel **Kenney**
Christopher Kimbley

George W. Kinney
Edward Kirwin
Edward Kiser
Benjamin F. Lee
Adrian Lucas
Thomas Lyons
Edward Maloney
Stephen Markham
Hugh McGowen
Alexander McMillen
Patrick Meagher
Isaac Mellin
Henry C. Mereness
John Moles
Thomas Morgan
Levi Morway
David D. Moser
Edward McCann
John McManus
George Neeger
James O'Conner
William O'Grady
Jonathan Oliver
Andrew O'Neil
Albert Parker
George H. Patterson
Alonson Pearce
Martin Pringle
Patrick Quigley
Thomas Richards
William Riley
Joseph Robbe
Frank Schiffmacher
John L. Shackelford

Charles Shaile
Charles Shellhert
James M. Sivine
LaFayette G. Smith
David Stancleft
Edward N. Stewart
Edgar I. Town
Lewis Ward
Frank Watier
George Werner
George Whiting
Noah Wickersham
John Wilkie
Zule Witsel
Charles Wright
John Wyne

13th U. S. Infantry.

Sergeant-Major George W. Steever
First Sergeant Frank Dilworth
Sergeant James E. Browne
Charles H. Ludlow
John C. Matthews
Milo J. Somers
Jesse B. Webster
Corporal Edward Maher
Daniel T. Payne
Asahel Skinner
Robert H. Slate
Henry Yank
Musician George Haney
Private Richard Bailey
John Beringer
Jacob H. Bumgardner

Clark Burris
Thomas Cassidy
William H. Clair
Joseph C. Cramer
John Danaha
Thatcher O. Danforth
Alonzo S. Eaton
Dennis Flynn
John Gillespie
John Glancy
Edward Hamilton
John Hampson
William H. H. Harrison
Alfred Hastings
Asaph K. Hildreth
Christopher Hite
Anton Jeager
George H. Johnson
John C. Kimble
Augustus G. Laban
John Larner
Daniel Lienhardt
Henry Lurink
John Maggert
William Miller
Charles H. Mooers
James Nash
Richard H. Palmer
Frank Roberts
Gottfred Rocht
Charles Schroeder
William P. Sims
Thomas Warner
Charles Wheaton

Michael Winn
Edward D. Wood

14th U. S. Infantry.
First Sergeant Joseph Stengele
Sergeant John F. Barnes
John Doyle
John Collins
Albert Funke
Jesse A. Ingersoll
Francis L. Theremin
Albert M. Welles
James Williams
Thomas F. Wise
Corporal William H. H. Barnhart
Joel Edmund Benton
Francis Burchard
John Burke
Daniel Cavanagh
Lewis F. Colton
William A. Fay
Gustav Fomm
James Green
Milles Jamerson
John Laffin
George Meyers
William H. Reed
Augustus S. Vogintz
James Worrell
Private William U. Aid
John W. Allen
James A. Alexander
Abram Baker
Marion Bartholf

Lewis Berkfelt
John Bonaparte
William J. Boyle
Warner Brown
Edward Burns
Harrison Carkin
Samuel Carnes
Patrick Cassidy
Hiram Cole
Parker C. Colladay
George Compton
Patrick Cooney
Nathaniel B. Copp
Arthur Cosgrove
Paul S. Crosby
John Cushing
Gurdin B. Dart
John Davidson
Patrick Degnan
Thomas Diamon
Michael Donohue
William Driesbach
Dennis Driscoll
John M. Easby
James Eagin
Hector Fanton
John Farrell
Charles Fees
John Fitzgerald
John Foley
Henry Francis
Robert Franey
Dudley Gordon
James Gordon

Samuel W. Goodall
Frederick Grasper
John Green
Allen Hadley
William D. Hammonds
Thomas Hannah
William Harris
James Hart
Hiram Haynes
John C. Heath
Jackson Henion
Barney Horan
John L. Horton
Edmund W. Howard
Horace P. Howd
Andrew J. Hughes
John Jefferies
• William Jenner
Moses Jones
Henry Keast
Tracy A. Kellogg
Albert Kendall
Christopher Klenk
Duncan Langmuir
Patrick Larkin
Michael Ledwitch
Byron Loomis
Andrew Love
David Loyall
Charles Lucua
Martin Luhtz
Dennis Martin
Nicholas W. Millis
John McAlpine

Arthur McCune
John McDonald
Thomas McDonald
James McManus
John McSorley
Peter Millmore
James Minogue
Walter Moll
James Morrison
Thomas Murray
John Mooney
Thomas Mulligan
Hiram Newman
Thomas Noonen
Charles O'Conner
Patrick O'Neill
Edwin G. Osgood
Joshua Peck
Sidney R. **Peterson**
Charles N. Phillips
Patrick Power
William Prescott
Ezra **Prindle**
David Regan
Oliver Robbins
Hiram B. Robinson
Martin Roney
Charles Schirmer
Ozias Shank
Thomas E. Sheets
Richard Simpkins
Simon Singerling
George Slade
George Smith

Samuel S. Smith
John Smith
Henry Snider
George Stadler
Edson Stevens
Frederick Stevens
William H. Swartz
Robert Swindells
James Trusdell
George F. Turner
Ezra Vallean
Edward Vining
Mark Ward
George Watson
Sidney Way
John Weik
Erastus D. Woodman
Playford Woods

15th U. S. Infantry.
First Sergeant Edward Cummings
Charles Kelling
Sergeant William H. Benson
Peter Byrnes
Peter Hartz
John G. Hughes
John Kanable
Edward Quinn
Corporal Augustus Brown
Daniel Butler
John Carr
Charles Wesley Chessroun
Samuel T. Davis
J. Henry Ferris

AT WEST POINT

Thomas M. Irwin
William McDonald
Thomas Price
Musician Patrick Burns
Private Robert Adams
Mathias Akerman
Jacob Aumiller
John Bawer
Jonathan Blaker
Franklin Blanz
David Bowman
Chester Brown
Isaac Bubb
Archelaus Card
Joseph A. Cellar
Andrew J. Collins
William E. Coyn
John Cradle
Henry Darwood
Isaac Debore
Isaac Detwiler
Enoch Dunham
Andrew Duttry
Thomas Findly
Samuel Finley
Elias Fissel
Patrick Fits
John Frank
Ithiner Gatton
Benjamin Geph
Gustave Gericke
Peter Gilooly
Jesse B. Goodsell
Elias K. Gruver

David Hartz
William M. Hatch
Henry M. Hayden
Lawrence Hayes
Thomas Hegan
William Hennicy
Jacob Hexamer
Edward Higley
William H. Hoover
Robert M. Horner
Robert Howell
Vincent Jester
David Jones
William Kappel
William Ambrose King
Harrison Kinney
Emanuel Kritzer
Joseph T. R. Lamb
William Leiby
James H. Lemon
Francis M. LeRoy
Isaiah Lomison
John Marrs
John Marshall
John W. Marshgrove
Christian F. Matznick
John Mauk
Samuel Mehaffey
Franklin Meson
John Murphy
William McCall
Florence McCarty
James H. McDowell
Daniel McGowan

James McKinley
Robert Miller
Edward Moran
Michael McCabe
Patrick McDonald
Daniel Neely
Samuel Newcomb
Cyrus Newman
Jeremiah Nichols
Samuel G. Nunveller
Joshua W. Patten
David Perry
Joshua M. Prevost
Farrel Queenan
Suton B. Quin
Robert Raison
Alex. C. Ramsey
Daniel Reichart
Josephus Reis
Benjamin Riddle
Edward Rogers
Hamilton W. C. Roney
Newton Root
John Rourke
Robert Ruttman
Joseph Sandbach
Benjamin Scott
Thomas J. Scutt
Philip Sep
Harrison C. Smith
Jesse Sponsler
Joseph Styer
Thomas Suthers
Martin V. Suttle

John Sweaney
Henry Symington
Charles W. Thompson
George Townsend
Charles H. Umbaugh
Lewis Vasion
Gustavus Vincent
John Walsh
William E. Walter
Harrison Wannamacher
John Waugh
Thomas E. Whiteside
David Wise

16th U. S. Infantry.
Commissary Sergeant James M. Howe
Sergeant Brice Veirs Baker
William D. Reynolds
Corporal Thomas Donahue
David C. Jennings
Alexander Kinkaid
Thomas O'Neill
Robert Robinson
Cortland Wells
Private Samuel C. Adams
Walter F. Amos
Hallett W. Barber
Alexander Boyle
Edward Brady
Amos Brainard
James Brooks
James Buck
Thomas Caldwell
Patrick Canon

Erastus Cheedle
Frank Clark
Jacob Clement
Christian Corai
John Crabtree
Solomon H. Curtis
James Darcy
Gregory Drouillard
John Dubi
Fernando Ferguson
Carl Fjetterstrom
Nathan Frost
George E. Galligher
James Gillick
Francis A. Gilson
Nicholas Ginsburg
Nicholas Growney
John Harrison
Joseph Harper
Nicholas Hendelong
William J. Hendrickson
Martin Herrix
William Howard
John Hurley
George P. Hutchinson
Frederick Kalenbach
Patrick Keho
Michael Kilmartin
William J. Leslie
Benjamin Lewis
James B. Lewis
Hugh Livingston
Charles Lyons
George Mahon

Charles A. Mann
Amos Mellott
Elias Minnich
Patrick Murphy
Felix McCarthy
Patrick McCaughy
John McLeod
Martin O'Connor
John Olson
Louis Orth
Dennis O'Sullivan
Thomas Owens
Charles Page
Lemuel K. Palmer
Ami Curtis Perry
Robert Pitts
George L. Pooler
Samuel Robinson
Robert W. Russell
James Saunders
Warren E. Sawyer
Coleman Shuff
Benjamin F. Silsby
Aaron Simons
Richard Stanley
Charles B. Stiteler
Hanson Stocdal
John Stokes
Samuel Swainbank
Wilford Trueblood
Valentine Vigar
Charles West
Zacariah G. White
John Williams

17th U. S. Infantry.

First Sergeant William H. T. Hogan
Sergeant Silas P. Blanchard
James M. Downs
Charles P. Giles
Henry P. Hyde
Henry J. Madison
Ransom L. Smith
Corporal Stephen G. Armstrong
Elias H. Baker
John Elliott
Dennis Fitzpatrick
Francis D. Gould
James Mitchell
John S. Pomeroy
John W. M. Small
John C. Wadsworth
Lester F. Wells
Private Albion T. E. Avery
Albert I. Allard
William F. Banks
Patrick Baron
Enos S. Bishop
Thomas Brozzen
David Burke
Charles P. Butler
William A. Byrne
William Cahill
Washington Cole
Daniel J. Conant
Solon L. Cornell
William J. Cottell
David Crider
William Duffy

Alphonso Estes
John Finton
Patrick Flood
Frederick W. Gans
Albert M. Gould
Michael Hallinan
George G. Hammond
Joseph Henny
Ephraim Holmes
Edwin A. Howard
Rufus B. Jameson
Thomas Kearney
George M. Kennerson
Louis Kilborn
Marcus Killam
John King
Michael King
Michael Landers
Nathaniel Lombard
Thomas Lynn
James Mangan
Michael Marshal
Patrick Mehan
James Merrill
Charles H. Miller
Jacob Mitchell
Michael Murphy
Samuel Murray
James McHough
John McMahon
Barney McNamee
Erskine E. McMillan
Amos Newland
Stover W. Nichols

Patrick O'Brian
Bartholomew O'Donnell
Michael O'Kane
George W. Paul
William Pender
Robert Perkins
Orlando H. Powers
Joseph Prince
George C. Prouty
William Schmidt
Fairy Selem
Sebastian Shaffer
George Sites
Carl Joseph Standar
Benjamin Stone
Edward Sullivan
Charles H. Temple
Henry Thompson
Isaac Travis
Josiah Victory
Charles H. Whitney
Constantine Yeker

18th U. S. Infantry.
Sergeant-Major Christopher Peterson
First Sergeant Zenas Dunham
Ruggels Elrick
George F. White
Sergeant James Barrett
John G. Boyce
Cheyney H. Dawson
Samuel Dobbins
Amos Flegal
Solomon Greenley

Henry Headley
Thomas W. Jesse
William P. Leibole
William D. Madeira
Thomas Shonessy
William Tombon
Tunis H. Swick
Joseph F. Wether
Corporal Jesse H. Brooks
Bernard C. Connelly
Joseph H. Dodds
John C. Donnelly
Warren D. Estabrook
John Falter
Alexander Goodwell
Joseph L. Harcourt
William H. Himes
Samuel Hobill
Jacob Leibole
John Linebaugh
Isaac Linn
Thomas J. Long
James Lowden
Engelbert A. Miller
Uriah H. McDowell
Patrick O'Connors
Francis M. Philippi
William Walter
Musician James Marsh
Private James Adair
John Alberty
Peter Altmeyer
James Anderson
James A. Anderson

Charles Argus
S. T. Armstrong
John W. Arthur
William Baglin, Jr.
Gordon Beard
Ezra Beckwith
William H. Bellfield
Isaac Bemesdarfer
Edwin Benjamin
Andrew Bowers
Jacob Bike
Jacob Blessing
Joseph Bray
Bernard Brinck
George Brooks
Preston Brown
Henry Burns
Martin Burr
George W. Burton
Adolphus Caio
Arthur D. Cantrell
John J. Carmean
John Cashiell
John W. Cass
Bishop Church
Miller Clark
Abraham Combs
Andrew J. Connor
William Cornwall
William H. Crandall
Edward Cunningham
Samuel Daihl
Thomas B. Daniels
Alexander Dean

Thompson J. W. Devor
William H. Diehl
James Dixon
William Durller
George Eckert
Joseph F. Elcbeck
William Ennis
Joseph A. Ensign
Valentine Farrenkoff
James S. Fisher
James Fitzgerald
Willis B. Fitzgerald
Franklin S. Frick
John Fussalmann
Michael Gallivin
Philip Gorsuck
William Gray
Mahlon F. Hancock
James Handley
Elisha Harper
James Harrisson
John T. Havice
Jarret Claiborn Headington
Alexander Helmold
Moses C. Helvirson
Ambrose Higgins
Ferdinand Hill
Samuel Hill
Nicholas Holsbach
Joseph Hook
Jeremiah Howald
George W. Hoyt
Thomas Porter Hunley
W. W. Hutchison

Joseph A. Hynus
John Jacobee
Joel Jacobs
John Jewel
Isaac B. Jones
Richard J. Jones
Frank Kelley
Fredric H. Kiest
George W. Kleckner
Daniel Kring
Edward P. Lacey
Charles W. Laff
Michael Larkin
William H. Larrowe
Anthony Livingston
Joseph Luken
James B. Massey
Francis Masterson
John Merten
Thomas Mooney
George H. Morrison
Samuel Mowrer
Patrick McDonnell
Peter Murphy
James W. McAdow
Alfred M. McGinnis
Robert McGuire
Thomas Nary
Robert F. Nightingale
Dennis O'Brien
James O'Neill
John O'Hara
James Ostrander
Samuel Palmer

John W. Parsons
Thornton Perry
Harvey Peters, Jr.
John W. Peters
William L. Pinney
Emery Plumley
George H. Poorman
Timothy Quinn
Martin Rapstock
Nathan Ray
Stephen Ray
David Redmon
Charles Reifenberg
Samuel C. Rhoads
Henry Rider
Charles Roberson
William H. Robey
Amos Robins
Patrick Savage
Joseph W. Sawyer
James M. Saxton
Theodore Schmitz
Charles Schreck
Hugh Scolan
Gideon W. B. Searight
Jacob Shaffer
Amos Sherman
Isaac S. Shoffner
Christian Shrack
George Shuler
William Sieg
Joseph Harrison Silk
George B. Smith
Harrison D. Smith

Henry D. Smith
James Smith
John M. Smith
David Sours
George W. Stierhof
David D. Stine
George W. Stone
Francis Stoufer
George W. Stover
Martin V. Swank
William H. Swisher
Abraham Tabler
Jonas Tallhamer
Newton Tharp
William H. Thomas
James Thompson
John Henry Tieman
Jonathan Trueblood
George Waterfield
Alexander White
William E. Wilison
Isaac Wilson
John Wilson
Joseph Wosmer
Franklin Zimmerman

19th U. S. Infantry.
Sergeant James F. Day
Patrick Leonard
John H. Topky
Corporal Lewis Bols
Nicholas Clemenz
Benjamin Davis
Thomas Doyle

Joseph Furer
Frederick Kunzel
John Reed
Alexander Van Dolkum
John R. Waller
Private John W. Barnes
John Boyer
Thomas Brennen
Charles Brown
David M. Chubb
John Dignan
Townsend E. Fall
Alexander Filson
Michael P. Fishell
David Gifford
George Goettinger
Edward Gorman
Bernard Haggerty
Joseph Hendricks
Samuel C. Higgins
Alexander Hood
Peter Laughlin
Aaron Luther
Patrick Lynch
William Manning
George W. McGuinn
John O'Brien
James Pierson
Henry Porter
John Quinn
William Randall
William Resor
Jacob Romig
John Schilbe

Philip Schrom
Henry Shul
Adam Smith
James Smith
Claiborne Taliafero
Charles Tanner
Paul Tatem
Henry Thompson
Henry T. Tibbits
John Wilger

RECAPITULATION.

Total number of officers killed . . . 188
Total number of enlisted men killed . . 2042

OFFICERS.

General Officers . . . 2
General Staff Officers . . 4

Staff Corps.

Corps of Engineers 7
Corps of Topographical Engineers . . 2
Ordnance Department 2

                          Total Staff Corps   11

Cavalry.

1st Cavalry	.	8	4th Cavalry . .	5
2d Cavalry	.	5	5th Cavalry . .	8
3d Cavalry	.	2	6th Cavalry . .	8

                          Total Cavalry   36

Artillery.

1st Artillery . .	8	4th Artillery . . 6
2d Artillery . .	5	5th Artillery . . 10
3d Artillery . .	3	
		Total Artillery 32

Infantry.

1st Infantry .	2	11th Infantry . 8
2d " .	9	12th " . 11
3d " .	2	13th " . 4
4th " .	4	14th " . 10
5th " .	3	15th " . 4
6th " .	2	16th " . 9
7th " .	4	17th " . 9
8th " .	3	18th " . 9
9th " .	0	19th " . 4
10th " .	6	
		Total Infantry 103

ENLISTED MEN.

Staff Corps.

Battalion of Engineers	2	Signal Corps . 6
Ordnance Corps .	1	General Service . 1
		Total Staff Corps 10

Cavalry.

1st Cavalry .	79	4th Cavalry . 42
2d " .	72	5th " . 52
3d " .	26	6th " . 47
		Total Cavalry 318

THE BATTLE MONUMENT

Artillery.

1st Artillery	. 76	4th Artillery	.	80
2d "	. 48	5th "	.	81
3d "	. 39			
		Total Artillery		324

Infantry.

1st Infantry .	. 31	11th Infantry	.	115
2d " .	. 87	12th " .	.	118
3d " .	. 37	13th " .	.	52
4th " .	. 51	14th " .	.	150
5th " .	. 16	15th " .	.	129
6th " .	. 31	16th " .	.	87
7th " .	. 47	17th " .	.	89
8th " .	. 13	18th " .	.	205
9th " .	. 0	19th " .	.	51
10th " .	. 81			
		Total Infantry		1390

LIST OF ORIGINAL SUBSCRIBERS FOR THE BATTLE MONUMENT.

Name and Rank.	Amount.
Abbot, H. L., Captain of Engineers	$13.00
Abert, J. W., Major of Engineers	10.00
Alderdice & Co., Sutlers, 12th Infantry	10.00
Aldrich, B., Lieutenant 8th Infantry	7.00
Alexander, C. T., Surgeon	10.00
Alexander, E. B., Colonel 10th Infantry	13.00
Ames, A., Brigadier-General; Lieutenant 5th Artillery	18.00
Ames, E. R., Lieutenant 7th Infantry	10.00
Amory, T. J. C., Col. Mass. Vols.; Capt. 7th Infy.	13.00
Anderson, T. M., Captain 10th Infantry	10.00
Andrews, C. C., Colonel 3d Minn. Volunteers	13.00
Arnold, A. K., Captain 5th Cavalry	10.00
Arnold, Isaac	7.00
Arnold, W. F., Lieutenant 8th Infantry	7.00
Ash, J. P., Captain 5th Cavalry	10.00
Atchison, C. B., Capt. A. D. C. Vols.; Lt. 3d Inf.	8.00
Austin, R. H., Capt. 24th Wisconsin Volunteers	10.00
Ayres, R., Lieutenant 19th Infantry	10.00
Babbitt, L. S., 1st Lieutenant Ord. Department	10.00
Bache, H., Colonel of Engineers	13.00

Name and Rank.	Amount.
Bacon, C., Jr., Assistant Surgeon	$7.00
Baden, J. T., Lieutenant 5th Cavalry	10.00
Bailey, T. C. J., Captain 17th Infantry	10.00
Bainbridge, E. C., Captain 5th Artillery	8.00
Bainbridge, A. H., Lieutenant 14th Infantry	7.00
Baird, A., Brigadier-General	50.00
Baldwin, H. M., 2d Lieutenant 5th Artillery	10.00
Bales, F. H., Captain, retired	8.00
Ball, E., Lieutenant 1st Cavalry	7.00
Bankhead, H. C., Captain 5th Infantry	11.00
Barclay, C. B. (Citizen)	100.00
Barry, R. P., Captain 16th Infantry	8.00
Barry, W. F., Brig.-Gen., Major 5th Artillery	18.00
Bartholomew, W. H., Captain 16th Infantry	7.00
Bartlett, C. G., Captain 12th Infantry	10.00
Bartlett, W. H. C., Prof. U. S. M. A.	15.00
Beaumont, E. B., Captain 4th Cavalry	8.00
Beckwith, A., Major Subsistence Department	15.00
Beecher, H. B., Lieutenant 4th Artillery	10.00
Beecher, Rev. H. W.	50.00
Benét, S. V., Captain Ordnance Department	10.00
Benham, H. W., Brigadier-General Volunteers	18.00
Benjamin, S. N., Lieutenant 3d Artillery	10.00
Benton, J. G., Captain Ordnance Department	10.00
Best, C. L., Captain 4th Artillery	11.00
Bisbee, W. H., Lieutenant 18th Infantry	7.00
Bliss, A., Captain and A. Q. M.	20.00
Blunt, C. E., Major Engineers	10.00
Blunt, M. M., Captain 12th Infantry	8.00
Board, C. A. F., retired	8.00
Bomford, J. V., Lieutenant-Colonel 16th Infantry	11.00
Bonneville, B. L. E., Colonel, retired	13.00
Bowman, A. H., Colonel of Engineers	40.00

Name and Rank.	Amount.
Boyce, P., Lieutenant 8th Infantry	$10.00
Brackett, A. G., Colonel Vols.; Major 1st Cavalry	13.00
Brady, G. K., Lieutenant 14th Infantry	7.00
Brainerd, T. C., Assistant Surgeon	10.00
Brewerton, H., Lieutenant-Colonel of Engineers	25.00
Brigham, E. D., Capt. Com. Sub.	8.00
Britton, T., Lieutenant 6th Infantry	7.00
Brooks, W. T. H., Major-General	30.00
Brown, F. H., Lieutenant 18th Infantry	7.00
Brown, H., Lieutenant 18th Infantry	7.00
Buchanan, R. C., Lieut.-Colonel 14th Infantry	11.00
Buell, D. C., Major-General Volunteers	30.00
Buffington, A. R., Captain Ordnance Department	10.00
Burbank, S. W., Captain 14th Infantry	10.00
Burke, D. W., Lieutenant 2d Infantry	10.00
Burke, P. E., Captain 14th Infantry	8.00
Burnett, R. L., Lieutenant 12th Infantry	7.00
Burnham, H. M., First Lieutenant 4th Artillery	25.00
Burns, T., Lieutenant 1st Cavalry	10.00
Burns, W. W., Brigadier-General	18.00
Burroughs, Geo., Lieutenant Engineers	10.00
Bush, E. G., Captain 10th Infantry	8.00
Butler, J., Lieutenant 2d Infantry	7.00
Butterfield, D., Major-General	27.00
Byrne, T., Lieutenant 2d Infantry	7.00
Callender, F. D., Major Ordnance Department	10.00
Canby, S., Lieutenant 4th Artillery	7.00
Card, B. C., Captain and A. Q. M.	8.00
Carlin, W. P., Brigadier-General	20.00
Carney, J. D., Captain 17th Infantry	8.00
Carpenter, A. B., Lieutenant 19th Infantry	10.00
Carpenter, T. H., Captain 17th Infantry	8.00
Carr, C. C. C., Lieutenant 1st Cavalry	10.00

Name and Rank.	Amount.
Carr, E. A., Brigadier-General	$18.00
Carter, J. W., Lieutenant 17th Infantry	7.00
Casey, Silas, Major-General	30.00
Casey, T. L., Major Corps of Engineers	10.00
Chaffee, C. C., Lieutenant Ordnance Department	15.00
Chambers, A., Brigadier-General; Capt. 18th Infantry	20.00
Chambliss, W. P., Major 4th Cavalry	10.00
Chapman, W., Lieutenant-Colonel, retired	11.00
Chevers, M. L., Chaplain, U. S. A.	8.00
Choisey, G. L., Lieutenant 14th Infantry	7.00
Clarke, F. M., Captain 5th Artillery	10.00
Clay, H. DeB., Captain 14th Infantry	8.00
Clay, J. K., Lieutenant 14th Infantry	7.00
Clements, B. A., Surgeon	10.00
Clinton, Wm., Captain 10th Infantry	10.00
Coates, E. M., Lieutenant 12th Infantry	10.00
Coggswell, M., Captain 8th Infantry	10.00
Cole, A. A., Lieutenant 7th Infantry	7.00
Coleman, R. W., Civilian	15.00
Collins, G. H., Civilian	10.00
Comly, C., Lieutenant Ordnance Department	20.00
Comstock, C. B., Captain Corps of Engineers	11.00
Conrad, J. S., Captain 2d Infantry	8.00
Coolidge, R. H., Medical Inspector	15.00
Cooper, S. W., Lieutenant 8th Infantry	7.00
Coppinger, J. J., Captain 14th Infantry	10.00
Cornick, W. F., Assistant Surgeon	7.00
Counselman, J. H., Lieutenant 1st Artillery	10.00
Crilly, F. J., Captain and A. Q. M.	10.00
Crofton, R. E. A., Captain 16th Infantry	8.00
Crosman, C. H., Colonel and Quartermaster	13.00
Cross, O., Lieutenant-Colonel and Quartermaster	15.00
Culbertson, S. S., Lieutenant 19th Infantry	10.00

Name and Rank.	Amount.
Curtis, A., Lieutenant 19th Infantry	$10.00
Curtis, S. R., Major-General	27.00
Cushing, H. C., Lieutenant 4th Artillery	10.00
Cuyler, J. M., Surgeon U. S. A.	15.00
Dallis, A. J., Captain	10.00
Darling, J. A., Major Vols.; Lieut. 2d Artillery	10.00
Davidson, J. W., Brigadier-General	18.00
Davis, O. E., First Lieutenant of Engineers	7.00
Davis, R., Lieutenant 2d Infantry	7.00
Davis, T., Lieutenant 19th Infantry	10.00
Dean, W., Lieutenant 1st Cavalry	10.00
DeCourcy, F. E., Lieutenant 13th Infantry	10.00
DeKay, D., Lieutenant 14th Infantry	7.00
Delafield, R., Colonel of Engineers	50.00
Denton, A. B., 18th Infantry	10.00
DeRussy, R. E., Colonel of Engineers	25.00
Dimmick, J., Colonel U. S. A.	13.00
Dodge, R. I., Captain 8th Infantry	10.00
Dolan, M., Lieutenant 2d Infantry	10.00
Donaldson, J. L., Major Q. M. Department	15.00
Dorman, O. M., Paymaster Volunteers	10.00
Doubleday, A., Major 17th Infantry; Major-General	27.00
Downey, G. M., Lieutenant 14th Infantry	8.00
Dowling, J. T., Lieutenant 17th Infantry	7.00
Drouillard, J. P., Captain 6th Infantry	8.00
Drum, W. F., Captain 2d Infantry	8.00
Drummond, Thos., Captain 5th Cavalry	10.00
Drury, T., Lieutenant 2d Infantry	7.00
Dryer, H., Captain 4th Infantry	8.00
DuBarry, B., Major and Com. Sub.	10.00
DuBois, J. V., Captain 3d Cavalry; Col. of Vols.	13.00
Dudley, J. S., Lieutenant 2d Artillery	7.00
Duer, E. A., Lieutenant 1st Artillery	10.00

Name and Rank.	Amount.
Duncan, T., Major 3d Cavalry	$10.00
Dunn, T. S., Lieutenant 10th Infantry	10.00
DuPont, H. A., Lieutenant 5th Artillery	7.00
Dutton, A. H., Lieutenant of Engineers	15.00
Earle, M., Lieutenant 10th Infantry	10.00
Eckert, G. B., Lieutenant 3d Infantry	7.00
Eddy, A. R., Captain and A. Q. M.	8.00
Edgerton, W. G., Captain 11th Infantry	8.00
Edie, J. R., Lieutenant Ordnance Department	10.00
Edson, T., Captain Ordnance Department	8.00
Edwards, D., Lieutenant 19th Infantry	10.00
Egbert, H. C., Lieutenant 12th Infantry	10.00
Eggemeyer, A., Lieutenant 10th Infantry	10.00
Elder, S. S., Captain 1st Artillery	8.00
Elliot, G. H., Captain of Engineers	20.00
Elliott, W. L., Brigadier-General; Major 1st Cav.	20.00
Ellis, H. A., Captain 17th Infantry	10.00
Emerson, J. J., Lieutenant 17th Infantry	7.00
Estes, C. A. M., Lieutenant 16th Infantry	10.00
Evans, A. W., Captain 6th Cavalry	10.00
Ewers, E. P., Lieutenant 19th Infantry	7.00
Falk, W., Lieutenant 2d Infantry	7.00
Falvey, J., Lieutenant 3d Cavalry	7.00
Farley, J. P., Lieutenant of Ordnance	7.00
Farquhar, F. U., Captain of Engineers	8.00
Feiler, N. J., Captain 1st Cavalry	10.00
Fessenden, F., Col. Vols.; Capt. 12th Infantry	13.00
Fetterman, W. J., Captain 18th Infantry	8.00
Field, J. H. V., Lieutenant Ordnance Department	7.00
Fitzgerald, J., Lieutenant 2d Artillery	7.00
Fitzhugh, C. L., Lieutenant 4th Artillery	10.00
Flagler, D. W., Captain Ordnance Department	10.00
Fletcher, C. H., Captain 1st Infantry	8.00

Name and Rank.	Amount.
Flint, F. F., Lieutenant-Colonel	$15.00
Foot, A., Lieutenant 14th Infantry	7.00
Forsyth, J. W., Captain 18th Infantry	10.00
Foster, J. G., Major-General	30.00
Frank, R. T., Captain 8th Infantry	10.00
Franklin, W. B., Major-General; Col. 12th Infantry	30.00
Franklin, W. S., Captain 12th Infantry	8.00
French, W. H., Major-General	30.00
Fry, J. B., Major, A. A. G., Prov. Mar. General	13.00
Gansevoort, H. S., Lt. 5th Art.; Col. N.Y. Vol. Cav.	13.00
Gapen, H. C., Lieutenant 15th Infantry	7.00
Gardiner, J. W. T., Major, retired	10.00
Garrard, K., Brigadier-General; Captain 5th Cavalry	20.00
Gentry, W. T., Captain 17th Infantry	10.00
Getty, T. M., Surgeon	10.00
Gibbon, J., Brigadier-General	20.00
Gibbs, J. S., Lieutenant 1st Artillery	7.00
Gibbs, T. K., Lieutenant 1st Artillery	7.00
Gibson, A. A., Major 2d Artillery	10.00
Gibson, H. G., Col. of Vols.; Major 3d Cavalry	13.00
Giddings, G. R., Major 14th Infantry	10.00
Gilbert, C. C., Major 19th Infantry	10.00
Gillespie, G. L., Lieutenant of Engineers	10.00
Gillmore, Q. A., Major-General	27.00
Gilman, J. H., Captain and Com. Sub.	8.00
Goddard, C. C., Captain 17th Infantry	10.00
Goddard, C. E., Assistant Surgeon	7.00
Goodhue, J. M., Captain 11th Infantry	8.00
Gooding, O. P., Capt. 10th Inf.; Col. 6th Mass. Cav.	13.00
Gordan, G. H., Brig.-Gen. (late Capt. M. Rifles)	25.00
Graham, J. D., Colonel of Engineers	20.00
Granger, G., Major-General	27.00
Granger, R. S., Brigadier-General	20.00

Name and Rank.	Amount.
Grant, U. S., Lieutenant-General	$50.00
Greene, J. D., Colonel 8th Infantry	20.00
Greene, O. D., Major, A. A. G.	10.00
Green, M. C., Lieutenant 13th Infantry	10.00
Grier, W. N., Lieutenant-Colonel 1st Cavalry	11.00
Grossman, F. E., Lieutenant 7th Infantry	8.00
Haight, E., Captain Vols.; Lieutenant 16th Infantry	10.00
Haines, T. J., Colonel, Com. Sub.	13.00
Hall, J. A., Lieutenant 1st Cavalry	10.00
Hall, R. H., Captain 10th Infantry	20.00
Hall, R. M., Lieutenant 1st Artillery	7.00
Hamilton, J., Captain 3d Artillery	8.00
Hamilton, S. M., Lieutenant 3d Infantry	7.00
Hammond, J. F., Surgeon	10.00
Harbach, A. A., Lieutenant 11th Infantry	10.00
Hardin, M. D., Lieut.-Col. Vols.; Lieut. 3d Art'y	30.00
Hargrave, R. W., Lieutenant 17th Infantry	7.00
Harker, C. G., Captain 15th Infantry	13.00
Harrington, G., Lieutenant 3d Cavalry	7.00
Harris, W. H., Captain Ordnance	10.00
Haskin, J. A., Major 3d Artillery	12.00
Hastings, J., Lieutenant 5th Cavalry	10.00
Hawkins, H. S., Captain 6th Infantry	10.00
Hawkins, J. P., Brig.-Gen., Capt., and A. C. S.	50.00
Hawley, W., Lieutenant 3d Cavalry	7.00
Hay, C. E., Lieutenant 3d Artillery	12.00
Haymond, H., Captain 18th Infantry	10.00
Hazen, H. E., Lieutenant 8th Infantry	7.00
Head, J. F., Surgeon	10.00
Hearn, J. H., Lieutenant 16th Infantry	10.00
Hecksher, J. G., Captain 12th Infantry	10.00
Heilman, W. H., First Lieutenant 15th Infantry	7.00
Heintzelman, S. P., Major-General	30.00

Name and Rank.	Amount.
Hendrickson, T., Major U. S. A.	$10.00
Henley, J. P., Lieutenant 5th Artillery	8.00
Henry, G. V., Lieut. 1st Artillery ; Col. of Vols.	13.00
Hickox, C. R., Lieutenant 5th Artillery	10.00
Higbee, G. H., Lieutenant 11th Infantry	10.00
Hildeburn, S., Lieutenant 3d Cavalry	20.00
Hitchcock, E. A., Major-General	50.00
Hodges, H. C., Captain and A. Q. M.	10.00
Hoffman, Wm., Colonel 3d Infantry	15.00
Holden, L. H., Surgeon	10.00
Holman, Chas., Lieutenant 5th Artillery	7.00
Honey, S. A., Lieutenant 15th Infantry	7.00
Hooker, J., Major-General	27.00
Hope, L. F.	5.00
Hopkins, J. A., Lieutenant 17th Infantry	7.00
Hotsenpiller, C. W., Lieutenant 16th Infantry	7.00
Howard, C. O., Captain 18th Infantry	10.00
Howard, O. O., Major-General	27.00
Howard, R. V. W., Lieut.-Col. Vols.; Capt. 4th Art.	11.00
Howland, G. W., Captain 3d Cavalry	8.00
Hubbard, V. B., Assistant Surgeon	10.00
Hubbs, W. H., Lieutenant 13th Infantry	10.00
Hudson, E. McK., Captain 14th Infantry	10.00
Hunt, J. C., Lieutenant 1st Cavalry	10.00
Hunt, J. S., Lieutenant 4th Artillery	10.00
Huntington, H. A., Lieutenant 4th Artillery	10.00
Ilges, G., Captain 14th Infantry	8.00
Ingalls, R., Brigadier-General	18.00
Ingham, G. T., Lieutenant 11th Infantry	20.00
Ireland, D., Captain 15th Infantry	13.00
Irish, D. C., Captain 13th Infantry	8.00
Irvine, J. B., Lieutenant 13th Infantry	10.00
Irwin, B. J. D., Surgeon	10.00

Name and Rank.	Amount.
Jackson, J., Lieutenant 10th Infantry	$10.00
Jackson, R. H., Captain 1st Artillery	11.00
James, F. J., Lieutenant 3d Cavalry	20.00
Janeway, J. H., Assistant Surgeon	7.00
Johnson, J. B.	10.00
Johnson, G. W., Lieutenant 19th Infantry	7.00
Johnson, R. W., Brigadier-General	18.00
Jones, DeL. Floyd, Lieutenant-Colonel 19th Infantry	11.00
Kane, J. H., First Lieutenant 5th Artillery	10.00
Kurtz, J. D., Major of Engineers	10.00
Kellogg, E. R., Lieutenant 16th Infantry	7.00
Kellogg, J., Captain and A. C. S.	10.00
Kelton, J. C., Major and A. A. G.	20.00
Kendrick, H. L., Professor U. S. M. A.	20.00
Kennington, J., Lieutenant 11th Infantry	7.00
Kensel, G. A., Capt. 5th Art.; Lt.-Col. of Vols.	11.00
Kent, J. Ford, Capt. 3d Inf.; Lt.-Col. A. I. G.	11.00
Keteltas, H., Captain 15th Infantry	8.00
Keyes, E. D., Major-General; Colonel 11th Infantry	27.00
Keyes, H. W., Captain 14th Infantry	10.00
Kilburn, C. L., Lieutenant-Colonel and Com. Sub.	11.00
King, C. L., Captain 10th Infantry	10.00
King, W. R., Lieutenant of Engineers	7.00
Kingsbury, C. P., Major Ordnance Department	10.00
Kinzie, D. H., Lieutenant 5th Artillery	7.00
Kirtland, F. S., Lieutenant 18th Infantry	7.00
Knowlton, M., Captain, retired	8.00
Kress, J. A., Lieutenant Ordnance Department	7.00
Lacy, F. E., Lieutenant 2d Infantry	7.00
Lay, R. G., Captain 3d Infantry	8.00
Laidley, T. T. S., Major Ordnance Department	10.00
Lancaster, G., Lieutenant 17th Infantry	7.00
Lane, W. B., Captain 3d Cavalry	10.00

Name and Rank.	Amount.
Langdon, L. L., Captain 1st Artillery	$8.00
Lauman, G. S., Captain 10th Infantry	10.00
Larned, C. T., Paymaster	10.00
Latimer, A. E., Captain 11th Infantry	20.00
Leahy, M., Lieutenant 1st Artillery	7.00
LeConte, J. L., Surgeon	25.00
Leib, E. H., Captain 5th Cavalry	10.00
Leonard, H., Lieutenant-Colonel Pay Department	11.00
Lind, J. S., Lieutenant 18th Infantry	7.00
Lindsly, W., Assistant Surgeon	7.00
Livingston, L. L., Captain 3d Artillery	8.00
Long, E., Col. 4th Ohio Cavalry; Capt. 4th Cavalry	15.00
Long, J. W., Captain 2d Infantry	8.00
Lorentz, Antoine, Sword-Master U. S. M. A.	10.00
Lowell, C. R., Col. 2d Mass. Cav.; Capt. 6th Cav.	13.00
Lattimore, W. O., Lieutenant 19th Infantry	10.00
Lyman, G. H., Lieutenant-Colonel Medical Dept.	11.00
Lynn, D. D., Captain 6th Infantry	8.00
Lyster, W. J., Lieutenant 19th Infantry	10.00
Mack, O. A., Captain 13th Infantry	10.25
Macomb, J. N., Lieutenant-Colonel of Engineers	20.00
Maley, T. E., Lieutenant 5th Cavalry	10.00
Marcy, R. B., Colonel, Inspector General	13.00
Marshall, L. H., Major 16th Infantry, Col. of Vols.	13.00
Marye, W. A., Lieutenant Ordnance Department	10.00
Mason, E. C., Captain 17th Infantry	13.00
Mason, J. W., Captain 5th Cavalry	10.00
May, J. H., Lieutenant 10th Infantry	10.00
Maynadier, H. E., Captain 15th Infantry	10.00
Maynadier, W., Colonel Ordnance Department	15.00
McCall, C. A., Assistant Surgeon	7.00
McClellan, E., Assistant Surgeon	7.00
McClintock, J., Captain 14th Infantry	8.00

Name and Rank.	Amount.
McCook, A. McD., Major-General	$50.00
McCormick, C., Surgeon U. S. A.	10.00
McCrea, Tully, Lieutenant 1st Artillery	7.00
McDowell, I., Major-General	27.00
McFeely, R., Lieutenant-Colonel Com. Dept.	11.00
McGee, Lieutenant 13th Infantry	8.00
McGilvray, J., Lieutenant 4th Artillery	7.00
McGinniss, J. R., Lieutenant Ordnance Department	10.00
McKee, S., Captain 1st Cavalry	10.00
McKee, S. A., Captain 2d Infantry	8.00
McKeever, C., Major, A. A. G.	10.00
McKibbin, C., Lieutenant 14th Infantry	7.00
McKibbin, D. B., Lieutenant 14th Infantry	10.00
McKibbin, R. P., Captain 4th Infantry	7.00
McKibbin, Sutler 12th Infantry (citizen)	10.00
McKnight, J., Captain 5th Artillery	25.00
McLaren, A. N., Surgeon U. S. A.	10.00
McLaughlin, N. B., Captain 4th Cavalry	10.00
McLoughlin, G. H., Lieutenant 2d Infantry	7.00
McMullin, G. O., Lieutenant 3d Cavalry	7.00
McNally, C. H., Captain 3d Cavalry	8.00
McNutt, J., Captain Ordnance Department	10.00
Meade, G. G., Major-General	30.00
Meigs, J. R., Lieutenant of Engineers	10.00
Meigs, M. C., Brigadier-General, Q. M. General	20.00
Meinhold, C., Lieutenant 3d Cavalry	7.00
Meline, J. F., Colonel of Volunteers, A. D. C.	10.00
Mendenhall, J., Captain 4th Artillery	10.00
Merrill, L., Colonel of Volunteers, Captain 2d Cav.	13.00
Merrill, W. E., Captain of Engineers	10.00
Michie, P. S., Lieutenant of Engineers	7.00
Miles, Evan, Lieutenant 12th Infantry	10.00
Milhau, J. J., Surgeon U. S. A.	15.00

Name and Rank.	Amount.
Miller, J. F., Captain 14th Infantry	$8.00
Miller, M. S., Major and Quartermaster	10.00
Mills, M., Surgeon	10.00
Mills, W., Lieutenant 16th Infantry	7.00
Mills, W. H., First Lieutenant 14th Infantry	10.00
Monahan, D., Lieutenant 3d Cavalry	10.00
Montgomery, D. L., Captain 17th Infantry	10.00
Moody, G. C., Captain 19th Infantry	10.00
Mooney, J., Captain 19th Infantry	10.00
Mordecai, A., Captain Ordnance Department	10.00
Morehead, W. J., Captain 17th Infantry	10.00
Morgan, C. A., Colonel of Vols., 4th Artillery	13.00
Morgan, H. C., Lieutenant 10th Infantry	10.00
Morgan, M. R., Lieutenant-Colonel, Com. Sub.	11.00
Morris, L. O., Captain 1st Artillery	10.00
Morris, R. L., Captain 18th Infantry	10.00
Morris, L. T., Lieutenant 19th Infantry	10.00
Morrison, P., Colonel, retired	13.00
Mulhenberg, F. P., Captain 13th Infantry	10.00
Mulligan, J. B., Captain 19th Infantry	10.00
Myers, E., Lieutenant 1st Cavalry	10.00
Myers, F., Lieutenant-Colonel and Quartermaster	13.00
Myers, J., Lieutenant Ordnance Department	8.00
Myers, Wm., Quartermaster	13.00
Myrick, J. R., Lieutenant 3d Artillery	10.00
Nash, B. F., Lieutenant 5th Artillery	7.00
Nealy, O. H., Lieutenant 11th Infantry	7.00
Neill, T. H., Brigadier-General	18.00
Noble, H. B., Lieutenant 8th Infantry	10.00
Noggle, C. L., Lieutenant 2d Infantry	7.00
Norris, B., Surgeon	10.00
Norton, A. S., Major and A. D. C. Volunteers	18.00
Norton, G. D., Captain 14th Infantry	8.00

Name and Rank.	Amount.
Noyes, H. E., First Lieutenant 2d Cavalry	$10.00
Oakes, J., Lieutenant-Colonel 4th Cavalry	20.00
O'Beirne, R. F., Captain 14th Infantry	10.00
Ogden, F. C., Lieutenant 1st Cavalry	10.00
Ogden, R. L., Captain and A. Q. M.	8.00
Ostrander, J. S., Lieutenant 18th Infantry	7.00
Otis, E., Captain 4th Cavalry	8.00
Palmer, Innis N., Brigadier-General	18.00
Parke, J. B., Lieutenant 10th Infantry	7.00
Parke, J. G., Major-General	50.00
Parker, D., Captain 3d Infantry	10.00
Parker, R. C., Lieutenant 12th Infantry	10.00
Parry, E. R., Lieutenant 11th Infantry	10.00
Patterson, H. W., Lieutenant 4th Infantry	7.00
Patterson, J. H., Lieutenant 11th Infantry	7.00
Patterson, W. W., Lieutenant 10th Infantry	10.00
Paul, G. R., Lieutenant-Colonel 8th Infantry	11.00
Pease, W. B., Captain 17th Infantry	8.00
Pease, W. R., Captain 7th Infantry	8.00
Pennington, A. C. M., Lieutenant 2d Artillery	7.00
Penrose, W. H., Colonel of Vols.; Capt. 3d Inf.	15.00
Perkins, D. D., Captain 4th Artillery	10.00
Perry, D., Lieutenant 1st Cavalry	10.00
Pettee, L., Lieutenant 11th Infantry	10.00
Phelps, E., Lieutenant 19th Infantry	7.00
Phelps, J. E., Lieutenant 3d Cavalry	15.00
Phipps, F. H., Lieutenant Ordnance Department	7.00
Phisterer, F., Lieutenant 18th Infantry	7.00
Pike, H. L., Lieutenant 1st Artillery	7.00
Pineo, P., Lieutenant-Colonel Medical Department.	11.00
Pleasonton, A., Major-General	27.00
Pomeroy, C. C., Captain 11th Infantry	8.00
Pope, J., Major-General	50.00

Name and Rank.	Amount.
Porter, A. P., Lieut.-Colonel.; Capt. Sub. Dept.	$50.00
Porter, G. L., Assistant Surgeon	10.00
Porter, H., Captain Ordnance Department	16.00
Porter, R. H., Lieutenant 14th Infantry	7.00
Potter, J. A., Captain and A. Q. M.	8.00
Potter, J. H., Major 7th Infantry	13.00
Pratt, H. C., Major and Paymaster U. S. A.	10.00
Prescott, W. H., Captain 16th Infantry	20.00
Prime, N., Captain 17th Infantry	10.00
Prince, F. E., Captain 10th Infantry	10.00
Procter, J. L., Captain 18th Infantry	8.00
Purcell, J. H., Lieutenant 1st Infantry	7.00
Putnam, H. R., Captain 12th Infantry	10.00
Putnam, J. E., Lieutenant 12th Infantry	10.00
Pyne, C. M., Lieutenant 6th Infantry	12.00
Ramsey, W. R., Assistant Surgeon	7.00
Randall, B., Surgeon U. S. A.	10.00
Randol, A. M., Captain 1st Artillery	10.00
Randolph, J. T., Surgeon	10.00
Rankin, W. G., Captain 13th Infantry	10.00
Ransom, H. C., Lieutenant-Colonel, Q. M.	13.00
Rathbone, H. R., Captain 12th Infantry	10.00
Raynolds, W. F., Major Engineers	13.00
Reid, J. R., Lieutenant 10th Infantry	7.00
Reese, C. B., Captain Engineers	8.00
Reese, H. B., Paymaster	10.00
Reeve, I. V. D., Lieutenant-Colonel 13th Infantry	11.00
Remington, P. H., Lieutenant 8th Infantry	7.00
Reno, M. A., Captain 1st Cavalry	10.00
Reynolds, C. A., Captain and A. Q. M.	11.00
Reynolds, J. J., Major-General	30.00
Ricketts, J. B., Brigadier-General	25.00
Rittenhouse, B. F., First Lieutenant 5th Artillery	10.00

Name and Rank.	Amount.
Ritter, J. F., Col. 1st Miss. Cav.; Capt. 15th Inf.	$13.00
Robbins, K., Lieutenant 5th Cavalry	10.00
Robert, H. M., Captain of Engineers	8.00
Roberts, B. S., Brigadier-General	18.00
Roberts, J., Lieutenant-Colonel 4th Artillery	13.00
Robertson, C. S., Lieutenant 10th Infantry	10.00
Robins, R., Lieutenant 11th Infantry	10.00
Robinson, D., Lieutenant 7th Infantry	7.00
Robinson, S. S., Captain 10th Infantry	8.00
Rockwell, C. F., Lieutenant Ordnance Department	10.00
Rodney, G. B., Lieutenant 4th Artillery	10.00
Rollins, J. H., Lieutenant Ordnance Department	10.00
Rosecrans, W. S., Major-General	27.00
Rossell, W. H., Captain 10th Infantry	8.00
Rowley, G. A., Lieutenant 2d Infantry	7.00
Roy, J. P., Captain 2d Infantry	10.00
Royall, W. B., Captain 5th Cavalry	10.00
Rucker, D. H., Brigadier-General, Q. M. D.	20.00
Ruggles, G. D., Major and A. A. G.	13.00
Russell, C. S., Captain 11th Infantry	10.00
Russell, D. A., Brig.-Gen., Major 8th Infantry	18.00
Russell, G., Lieutenant 3d Artillery	20.00
Sachs, W., Lieutenant 3d Cavalry	10.00
Sacket, D. B., Colonel and Inspector-General	13.00
Sanders, W. W., Captain 6th Infantry	8.00
Sanger, J. P., Lieutenant 1st Artillery	7.00
Sutorius, Alex., Lieutenant 3d Cavalry	7.00
Saxton, R., Brigadier-General	18.00
Scammon, C. T., 9th Ill. Vol. Cav., A. D. C.	10.00
Schenck, P. V., Assistant Surgeon	7.00
Schiffler, J. K., Lieutenant 16th Infantry	7.00
Schuyler, P., Captain 14th Infantry	10.00
Schwan, T., Lieutenant 11th Infantry	10.00

Name and Rank.	Amount.
Sedgwick, J., Major-General	$27.00
Sellers, E. E., Lieutenant 10th Infantry	10.00
Seymour, T., Brig.-Gen.; Capt. 5th Artillery	18.00
Sheridan, P. H., Major-General	27.00
Shipley, A. N., Captain and A. Q. M.	20.00
Sidell, W. H., Lieutenant-Colonel 15th Infantry	12.00
Silliman, H. R., Assistant Surgeon	10.00
Silvey, W., Captain 1st Artillery	8.00
Simonson, J. S., Colonel	13.00
Simpson, J. H., Lieutenant-Colonel of Engineers	11.00
Sinclair, J. B., Lieutenant 14th Infantry	7.00
Sinclair, Wm., Lieut.-Col. of Vols.; Lt. 3d Art.	11.00
Sitgreaves, L., Lieutenant-Colonel of Engineers	15.00
Slidell, W. J., Captain 16th Infantry	8.00
Slocum, H. W., Major-General	27.00
Slonge, J. L., Lieutenant 10th Infantry	10.00
Small, M. P., Lieutenant-Colonel Sub. Dept.	11.00
Smalley, H. A., Captain 2d Artillery	8.00
Smedberg, W. R., Captain 14th Infantry	10.00
Smith, A. K., Assistant Surgeon	10.00
Smith, A. T., Captain 8th Infantry	10.00
Smith, E. W., Captain 15th Infantry	11.00
Smith, F. G., Lieutenant 4th Artillery	10.00
Smith, G. A., Bvt. Lieutenant-Colonel	10.00
Smith, G. W., Lieutenant 17th Infantry	7.00
Smith, H. E., Captain 12th Infantry	10.00
Smith, J. H., Lieutenant 2d Artillery	7.00
Smith, L., Lieutenant 5th Artillery	7.00
Snyder, C., Lieutenant 8th Infantry	10.00
Snyder, J. A., Lieutenant 3d Infantry	10.00
Sokalski, G. O., Lieutenant 2d Cavalry	7.00
Sommer, H., Lieutenant 2d Infantry	7.00
Stacey, M. H., Lieutenant 10th Infantry	10.00

Name and Rank.	Amount.
Stanley, Wm., Lieutenant 10th Infantry	$10.00
Steele, F., Major-General	27.00
Stephenson, J. M., Lieutenant 4th Artillery	10.00
Sternberg, G. W., Assistant Surgeon	7.00
Stevens, H., Medical Department	8.00
Stewart, C. S., Major of Engineers	12.00
Stonge, S. E., Lieutenant 16th Infantry	7.00
Strickland, L. S., Lieutenant 16th Infantry	7.00
Stimpson, F. E., Lieutenant 17th Infantry	7.00
Strode, E. C., Assistant Surgeon	7.00
Strong, G. O., Brig-Gen. (by Gen. B. F. Butler)	27.00
Sully, A., Brigadier-General	18.00
Summers, J. E., Surgeon	11.00
Sumner, E. V., Captain 1st Cavalry	10.00
Sumner, S. S., Lieutenant 5th Cavalry	10.00
Suydam, C. C., Assistant Adjutant-General	10.00
Swan, W. W., Lieutenant 17th Infantry	10.00
Swartwout, H. A., Lieutenant 17th Infantry	10.00
Sweet, W., Captain 17th Infantry	8.00
Sweitzer, N. B., Captain 1st Cavalry	30.00
Swift, E., Surgeon U. S. Army	10.00
Swords, T., Colonel Q. M. D.	13.00
Sykes, G., Major-General	40.00
Symington, J., Colonel Ordnance Department	13.00
Taggart, D., Major and Paymaster	10.00
Taliaferro, L., Military Store Keeper	8.00
Tardy, J. A., Captain of Engineers	10.00
Tayler, A. B., Lieutenant 5th Cavalry	10.00
Taylor, J. McL., Lieutenant-Colonel, Com. Sub.	11.00
Theaker, H. A., Lieutenant 16th Infantry	7.00
Thieman, A., Lieutenant 10th Infantry	10.00
Thom, G., Lieutenant-Colonel of Engineers	13.00

Name and Rank.	Amount.
Thomas, E., Lieutenant 4th Artillery	$10.00
Thomas, G. H., Major-General	30.00
Thomas, L., Jr., Captain 1st Artillery	20.00
Thomas, P. K., Lieutenant 3d Cavalry	7.00
Thompson, J. A., Captain 4th Cavalry	8.00
Thorpe, W. C., Captain 13th Infantry	10.00
Tidball, J. C., Captain 2d Artillery	10.00
Tidball, J. L., Captain U. S. A.	8.00
Tilford, J. G., Captain 3d Cavalry	8.00
Tillson, J., Captain 19th Infantry	10.00
Tilton, H. R., Assistant Surgeon	7.00
Tompkins, C. H., Captain and A. Q. M.	8.00
Tompkins, D. D., Colonel and Q. M.	13.00
Tonne, W. R., Lieutenant 19th Infantry	10.00
Torbert, A. T. A., Brig.-Gen. Vols. U. S. A.	20.00
Totten, J. G., Brigadier-General Engineers	20.00
Totten, J., Brigadier-General; Major J. G. Dept.	18.00
Townsend, F., Major 18th Infantry	10.00
Trowbridge, C. F., Captain 16th Infantry	8.00
Turner, J. W., Brigadier-General; Captain, Com. Sub.	20.00
Upham, J. J., Captain 6th Infantry	20.00
Upton, E., Colonel	13.00
Urban, G., Lieutenant 5th Cavalry	10.00
Urmston, J. D., Lieutenant 12th Infantry	8.00
Vance, D. M., Lieutenant 11th Infantry	10.00
Van der Slice, J. H., Lieutenant 14th Infantry	7.00
Van Horne, J. J., Captain 8th Infantry	20.00
Van Renselaer, C., Captain 13th Infantry	8.00
Vernon, G. R., Lieutenant 14th Infantry	7.00
Vogdes, I., Brigadier-General	18.00
Wagoner, J. J., Lieutenant 19th Infantry	10.00
Wagner, H., Lieutenant 11th Infantry	7.00

Name and Rank.	Amount.
Wagner, J. P., Lieutenant 10th Infantry	$10.00
Walker, J. H., Lieutenant 14th Infantry	7.00
Walker, T. W., Captain U. S. A.	10.00
Wall, R., Lieutenant 3d Cavalry	10.00
Ward, R. B., Captain 11th Pa. Vol. Cav.	10.00
Ward, R. J., Lieutenant 1st Cavalry	10.00
Warner, C. N., First Lieutenant 4th Artillery	7.00
Warner, L. H., Lieutenant 7th Infantry	10.00
Warner, J. M., Lieutenant 8th Infantry	7.00
Warren, G. K., Major-General	30.00
Weaver, H. E., Lieutenant 8th Infantry	10.00
Webb, A. S., Brigadier-General	20.00
Webster, W., Surgeon	7.00
Weeks, G. H., Captain and Quartermaster	12.00
Wessells, H. W., Brigadier-General	20.00
West, W., Lieutenant 2d Infantry	7.00
Wharton, H. C., Lieutenant of Engineers	10.00
Wheaton, F., Brigadier-General; Capt. 4th Cavalry	20.00
Wheeler, J. B., Captain of Engineers	8.00
Whipple, W. D., Brigadier-General	18.00
White, C. B., Assistant Surgeon	7.00
Whitely, R. H. K., Lieutenant-Col. Ord. Dept.	11.00
Whitney, S., Lieutenant 4th Artillery	10.00
Whittemore, J. M., Captain Ordnance Department	8.00
Wikoff, C. A., Lieutenant 15th Infantry	7.00
Wilkin, A., Captain 17th Infantry; Col. Vols.	13.00
Wilcox, J. A., Lieutenant 4th Cavalry	7.00
Williamson, R. S., Major of Engineers	10.00
Williams, G., Lieutenant 4th Infantry	7.00
Williams, G. A., Captain 1st Infantry	10.00
Williams, J., Lieutenant 15th Infantry	7.00
Williams, S., Brigadier-General	18.00

Name and Rank.	Amount.
Williams, T. C., Captain 19th Infantry	$8.00
Wilson, J. E., Lieutenant 1st Artillery	7.00
Wilson, R., Lieutenant 5th Cavalry	10.00
Wilson, R. P., Lieutenant 17th Infantry	7.00
Winthrop, F., Captain	10.00
Wister, F., Captain 12th Infantry	10.00
Wolverton, W. D., Assistant Surgeon	7.00
Wood, T. J., Brigadier-General; Colonel 2d Cavalry	20.00
Wood, W. H., Major 17th Infantry	10.00
Woodhull, A. A., Assistant Surgeon	7.00
Woodruff, C. A., Lieutenant 2d Artillery	7.00
Woodruff, D., Major 12th Infantry	10.00
Woodruff, I. C., Major of Engineers	10.00
Woodward, S. E., Lieutenant 15th Infantry	7.00
Wright, H. G., Brigadier-General	18.00
Wright, J. P., Assistant Surgeon	7.00
Yates, T., Captain 13th Infantry	10.00
Yorke, L. E., Captain 13th Infantry	10.00

ENLISTED MEN.

Cavalry.

Organization.	Amount.
5 enlisted men Capt. Drummond's recruiting party, $1.00 each	$5.00
80 enlisted men Cavalry Detachment, West Point.	113.00

Artillery.

Organization.	Amount.
7 N. C. O. and Enlisted men Batty. L, 4th Arty.	$7.00
Enlisted men 5th Artillery; by Lt. Hickox	6.00
" " Battery B, 1st Artillery	67.00
48 enlisted men Co. K, 2d Artillery	48.00
33 Enlisted men Battery D, 1st Artillery	33.00
40 " " " M, 2d "	52.00
Band, 1st Artillery	21.00

Infantry.

7 Enlisted men Washington rec. rndvz., $1.00 each	7.00
2 Corporals Lt. Grossman's rec. party, $1.00 each	2.00
Lt. Wuniston's rec. party (two men), $1.00 each	2.00
Enlisted men Co. D, 1st Batt. 11th Infantry	80.00
" " Co. G, " "	34.00
" " Co. B, " "	21.00
" " Co. C, " "	15.00
" " Co. E, " "	18.50
" " Co. F, " "	17.00
11 Enlisted men 10th Infantry; by Capt. Sellers	25.00
56 " " 14th Infantry	57.00
52 " " 17th Infantry	52.00
2d Infantry Band	13.00
Enlisted men 2d Infantry	24.50
Enlisted men 12th Infantry Band	11.00
112 Enlisted men 12th Infantry	130.25
Sergt. Minneman, Sergt. Kennedy, Pvt. McNamara, 8th Infantry	8.00
2 Enlisted men 12th Infantry; by Captain Wiston	3.00
15 " " 7th Infantry, Co. F	18.00

AT WEST POINT

Volunteers.

Organization.	Amount.
Pvt. L. S. Phillips, 1st Ohio V. A., for his friend Lt. Frank Work, 4th U. S. Cavalry	$7.00
Enlisted men Hd. Qrs. 1st Brig. 2d Div. 5th Army Corps	21.00

Staff.

Regulars, Watertown, Mass.	13.00
Bradford, G., Ord. Sergt.	5.00

A DESCRIPTION
OF THE
QUARRYING, WORKING, TRANSPOR-
TATION AND ERECTION
OF THE
SHAFT OF THE
BATTLE MONUMENT
AT WEST POINT

EDITED BY
EDWARD F. MINER

QUARRYING AND WORKING.

THE quarry from which the shaft of the monument was taken is located at Stony Creek, in the town of Branford, Connecticut. The quarry has been opened up and extensively operated for only about ten or twelve years, so that there is little of historical interest gathered about it, although several buildings of a monumental character in the central and eastern sections of the country have been built of granite taken from it.

The chief characteristic of the quarry is the ability to produce large stones; the out-croppings on the hill above the portion opened up show ledges of very great length, without seams. For a building in Boston there was furnished a platform twenty-two feet ten inches long, seven feet wide and one foot seven inches thick. Another instance of the ability to produce large stones was given when at a single blast a block twenty feet square and fifty feet long, without crack or seam, was dislodged from the ledge. This block, if properly cut up, would have furnished stone for nine shafts like the one in the Battle Monument.

In quarrying the block for the monument, a bench was cleared in the quarry, having the top, one side and one end entirely free, and with the other end freed from the ledge by a natural seam. A line was marked off on the top surface for a second side, and a set of holes for a blast drilled along this line with a steam-drill. To insure breakage from the blast to be in the exact line required, lewis-holes were drilled — *i. e.*, one hole is drilled vertically and one obliquely on either side, all drilled from the same position of the tripod of the steam-drill. The powder put into these holes for the blast was fired simultaneously with a battery, and cleared the block from the ledge, opening up a seam from the top surface to the natural seam below. The result was a block more than twice the size required for the shaft. A large slab was removed from the top of the block with wedges, and then, by the same process of wedging, a rectangular block of the necessary size to make the shaft was split off. After the block of stone was entirely free it was tipped from the ledge, carefully inspected and rolled from the quarry to a suitable place where it could be cut and polished.

This whole process of quarrying, and the magnitude of the undertaking, are very clearly illustrated in the accompanying cut (I), which is a copy of a photograph taken at the quarry while the men were at work on the block.

The working of the shaft involved no new problems in stone-cutting and polishing except such as pertained to its exceptional size. The usual method of cutting the shaft of a column involves the splitting off of the corners of the block with wedges, then using the point and the pene hammer and finishing the surface with the bush or patent hammer. The first process in polishing is the grinding of the surface of the granite with chilled shot, then with different grades of emery and finishing or glossing with putty powder. Chilled shot is the trade name for small globular particles of chilled cast-iron; it being made by blowing out a molten stream of cast-iron with a steam jet. The first of these processes is accomplished by rubbing the surface of the granite to be polished with a block

of cast-iron under which is placed the chilled shot. Because of their size and globular form, each individual shot presents an almost infinitesimal point of contact with the stone, the result being that a slight pressure on an infinitely small area breaks down the surface of the stone. The process of grinding with emery is exactly similar, except that different grades of emery are used and the process requires a greater length of time. The grinding with emery leaves the stone with a very smooth, even surface, but no polish. The polish or gloss is put on by rubbing with a piece of felting covered with putty powder.

With the above description of cutting and polishing granite, the problems in working the monument shaft come clearly to view. Without question, for all the processes of working, it was best to mount the shaft so that it could be revolved, and no effort was spared in devising a scheme for doing so, since it was fairly expected that better results could be obtained in a much shorter time than in any other way.

Where it was proposed to work the shaft a platform of heavy timbers was laid down, and the stone rolled on to the platform and blocked up. The ends were then squared up, and the corners roughly knocked off, thus bringing the stone to a condition where it was necessary to have it revolve.

The process up to this point is shown in the accompanying cut (II).

As soon as the ends of the stone were squared up, journals were bolted to it at the ends, and half-boxes in which the journals were to revolve were placed upon a crib-work of timber. These journals were 13″ in diameter, 18″ long, and were cast of refined iron on a face-plate two and one quarter inches thick and three feet eight inches in diameter. On the inner or stone side of the face-plate was cast a hub of the same size as the journal, projecting into the stone six inches. Each face-plate was fastened to the stone by fourteen 1¾″ stud bolts, which were set on a circle three feet in diameter. The bolts were set six inches into the stone, and for this six inches they were cut with a very coarse lag screw-thread; the part of the shank passing through the face-plate being plain, and the nut end having the standard V thread.

After a careful series of experiments on the testing-machine in the laboratory of the Worcester Polytechnic Institute to determine the best method of fastening the stud bolts to the stone, it was decided to set them in sulphur. This material was selected because it developed the greatest strength of any material experimented with, was easily worked, and the fastenings could be used immediately.

The method adopted for setting the journals in position on the ends of the stone was as follows: A zinc template the size of the face-plate was cut out, and the position of the bolts accurately spaced off on the proper pitch-line. This template was applied to the end of the stone, and the position of the bolt-holes marked on the stone. With a steam-drill, holes six and one quarter inches deep and two and one quarter inches in diameter were drilled in the end of the stone. From the zinc template a wooden template was made thick enough, so that when a bolt was placed in one of the holes it was held firmly at right angles to the face of the template. The wood template was then placed in the proper position on the end of the stone, and the bolts one by one put in position, so that they projected into the holes drilled into the stone. Through a specially prepared channel in the wood template, melted sulphur was run into the holes in the stone, surrounding the bolts, and thus fastening them firmly and accurately in place. The wood template was removed, and the iron face-plate with the journal slipped on in its place, the nuts put on the bolts, and the face-plate tightly screwed to position against wooden wedges placed between it and the stone.

At this point the most difficult part of setting the face-plates

was encountered. The axis of each of the journals must coincide exactly with that of the stone shaft, or when the shaft was revolved the journals would bear at the outer end for part of the revolution, and at the inner end for the remainder, and would not lie truly in their bearings. The face-plates were set in exact position by means of measurements from a system of horizontal wires stretched the whole length of the shaft and from plumb-lines of wire. After the plate was brought to an exact position it was firmly bolted in place, being held by the wood wedges about one quarter of an inch away from the face of the stone. The space between the stone and the face-plate and around the projecting hub was filled with melted sulphur, which, when cold, gave a true surface against which the face-plate could be bolted without unduly straining either bolts or face-plate.

As soon as the face-plates were bolted in position the shaft was lowered so that the journals rested in the half-boxes prepared for them on the timber crib-work. For the purpose of cutting, before the machinery was set up, the shaft was revolved by means of a tackle block hitched to the end of a rope wound several times around the shaft.

To get the correct profile for the use of the stone-cutters, a reverse template was made of wood, and hung on hinges just above the shaft in the vertical plane of its axis. When in use, the template was dropped down, and measurements taken between it and the surface of the stone; at other times it was swung up to one side.

The cut (III) shows the stone mounted on the journals and the cutting partially completed.

As a precaution against breakage, it was thought desirable, in designing the machinery for revolving the shaft, to arrange it in such a manner as to furnish some support for the shaft. To accomplish this, two wooden pulleys (cut IV) eight feet in diameter and one foot ten inches on centers were placed at the center of the length of the shaft, and one third of the weight carried by means of wire-ropes R running from them to the driving-gear above. This driving-gear and the part of the weight of the shaft borne by the ropes were carried by three trusses E, made of ten by twelve inch timber, which in turn were footed upon a trussed stringer H to distribute the load over a large area.

The main trusses E were braced by plank G, and connected on the top by twelve-inch caps. On these caps were placed eight draw-bar car springs C, two over each of the outer trusses, and four over the center. On these springs were placed two six by twelve inch timbers, which in turn carried three ten by twelve timbers placed at right angles, these latter acting as seats for four pairs of long wedges K by which the wire ropes between the pulleys I and the sheaves B were kept at the proper tension. Upon the wedges rested a strong timber frame carrying three boxes in which ran a six-inch steel shaft. To this shaft were keyed two sets of three sheaves B, from which approximately one third of the weight of the shaft was hung by means of six seven-eighths inch wire ropes. The shaft also carried a twelve-foot wood pulley A, which was belted through a counter-shaft to a fifty horse-power engine. At its outer end the shaft was supported by a movable bearing balanced by a counter-weight D of nine hundred pounds.

It will be noticed that the device of supporting the six-inch steel shaft on springs gave the required flexibility which was necessary to allow for the unevenness of motion in such temporary work. By experiment the modulus of the springs was ascertained, so that with a simple device, indicating the compression, it was possible to know very closely how much of the weight of the stone shaft was carried by the ropes at any time.

The ropes first used were made with the ordinary long splice, and great difficulty was experienced in the splice pulling out and the wires breaking where the strands were crossed in the splic-

ing. This difficulty was overcome by using grommets — *i. e.*, rings of rope made from single strands of wire. They were made in the following manner: A piece of wire rope the required length and size was cut off and formed into a ring with the ends simply butted together. A single strand from this rope was removed and another strand of the same size from a long coil wound in its place, a second strand was then removed, and the same strand as before wound in its place. This process was continued until the six strands of the original ring of rope had been removed and the new single continuous strand wound in their place. The result was a ring of rope made from a single continuous strand, with, of course, only two ends to tuck in. These ropes were forty-two feet long, and in wearing out stretched ten inches, the stretch being taken up with the wedges.

The first process in polishing, that of grinding with chilled shot, was accomplished by placing on the top of the shaft flat pieces of cast-iron, called planes, having the under side curved to fit the shaft. They were held in place, when the stone revolved, by an attached piece of board which rested against a stringer plank placed at the back of the shaft. While the shaft was revolving the chilled shot mixed with lime and water was thrown upon the surface, and, passing under the planes, ground the stone to an even surface. After the surface was reduced as much as possible with the chilled shot, the same process was used with emery, the finest of the emery leaving the surface very smooth and even. After the emery was washed off, the planes were covered with a thick felt, and putty powder mixed with water was put on. This finished the surface with a polish or gloss, and completed the process.

One shift of the machinery had to be made in order to polish the surface under the first position of the wood pulleys. This was accomplished by tying together and bracing all of the parts to be moved, and then sliding them bodily four feet six inches to a new position.

From careful measurements of the water used in the boilers, the cylinder pressure of the engine and the pull of the planes on the surface of the stone, it was ascertained that the maximum horse-power used was slightly under twenty. By testing with a spring balance it was found that the friction of the planes varied with the material used in grinding, and also with the amount of water on the surface of the stone at the time. The friction when grinding with shot averaged eleven per cent. of the weight of the plane, twenty-five per cent. with the emery, and thirty-five per cent. when glossing. The shaft was run at an average of six and one third revolutions per minute. The time taken for the different operations was: for chilled shot, thirty-eight hours; emery, fifty-six hours; and glossing, eight hours, for each different length of surface worked at any one time.

TRANSPORTATION.

THE casing or boxing of the shaft for transportation was planned with especial view toward facilitating the erection at the site of the monument. It consisted of four fourteen-inch square timbers for stringers, fitted to the profile of the shaft and placed at four points equidistant about its circumference. These timbers were connected and held firmly in place by a series of heavy bolts. In order to reduce the danger of breakage to the shaft during transportation to a minimum, the vertical sides of the square formed by these heavy timbers were trussed. The bolts of the trussing passed through the stringers and also through a cross timber placed under the shaft and fitted to it. This gave support to the shaft at five points intermediate between the bearing points on the car. The stringer timbers projected some four feet beyond the small end or top of the shaft, and between these were fitted four cross timbers. One set of two cross timbers were twelve inches square and were fitted carefully to the necking and top of the shaft, and bolted securely to the stringers. Diagonally through these cross timbers were passed ten two-inch eye-bolts, five on each timber, the eyes of all bolts meeting in a line through the center of the other set of cross timbers, which were placed at right angles to the first set. Between the eye-bolts were placed the straps for the tackle block, and then a two and one half inch steel rod was passed through the timber, eye-bolts and straps, thus forming the connection by which the column was lifted when erected.

At the large, or bottom, end the stringer timbers projected only one foot and eight inches. Here two cross timbers were fitted at the end of the shaft and bolted firmly to the stringers. The ends of the bottom stringers were notched to receive a twelve-inch timber twelve feet long, whose section was three quarters round and one quarter square. This timber was used as a hinge on which the shaft was brought to an upright position when erected at the site.

The cars used for transportation were the usual design of flat cars, but were quite low and built extra heavy in all their detail, the axle being five by eight inches. They were thirty-eight feet six inches long, and were built and used by a locomotive builder for carrying two elevated railroad locomotives.

The cars were prepared for the shaft by laying ten by ten timbers on the car body, which were two feet longer than the distance between the centers of the trucks. They were blocked up from the car body two inches at the ends and held from side deflection by separator blocks fastened to the car, and by long bolts passing through the outer timbers down through the bolster blocks of the truss rods. The object of these timbers was to transmit directly to the trucks a part of the weight of the shaft, thus relieving the car body and truss rods beneath of an excessive load. The timbers carried a load sufficient to deflect them the two inches of the blocking plus the deflection of the car body.

Across these ten by ten stringer timbers were placed flatwise two eight by twelve inch timbers bolted firmly to them. Similar timbers were fastened to the stringers of the casing to the shaft, and fitted so that the shaft rested in them. These two sets of timbers were placed at each end of the shaft, and on

each car, and formed the bearing on which the shaft rested in transportation. All of the timbers were shod with iron and the set under the large end of the shaft was arranged with a two-inch king-bolt. At the other end the bolster timbers on the car were longer, and heavy blocks, having their inner surface worked to a curve, were bolted to them. At this end there was no fastening between the bolster blocks, and the casing of the shaft was allowed to slide back and forth as the motion of the cars required on the different curves of the railroads.

Loaded as described, the shaft was transported by railroad without any accident whatever. The only annoyance during the trip was caused by the heating of the journals of the axles. There was little difficulty when the speed of the train was kept below ten miles an hour; above that, the journals would run for only a short time without heating badly. The heaviest loaded set of trucks was under the large end of the shaft, and with the weight of the car it carried approximately seventy-five thousand pounds.

The cut (V) shows the cars as they appeared ready for shipment, with the shaft protected from the weather by a canvas cover.

The journey from Stony Creek to West Point was made over the New York, New Haven and Hartford Railroad from Stony Creek to Hartford via Saybrook Junction; from Hartford to Fishkill on the Hudson by the New York and New England Railroad; across the Hudson to Newburg by boat; and from Newburg to West Point over the West Shore Road — a total distance of one hundred and ninety-one miles. The trip was made in thirteen days, with an actual running time of thirty-eight hours.

The transportation from the switch at the West Point station up the steep hill to the site of the monument on the parade ground was accomplished by laying a temporary track in short sections,— no particular difficulty being experienced except near the riding school, where a reverse curve of seventy-five and eighty-five feet radii on a twelve per cent. grade was encountered. Here the curve was so short that the car timbers had to be deeply cut to allow the wheels of the trucks enough swing to pass the sharp curve. The shaft was not removed from the cars until it was blocked up at the site of the monument ready for erection. The cars were made up to a convenient height on a crib-work of timbers.

The cuts (VI, VII) illustrate very clearly the method of transportation from the railroad switch to the site.

ERECTION.

THE erection of the shaft was the subject of quite as much thought and planning as any part of its handling, the difficulty being not only the handling of so great a load, but that it must be put in an upright position without any weight being allowed to come upon the lower edge, since that would very likely break out a piece from the shaft. A method of erection similar to that used in erecting the Egyptian obelisk in Central Park, New York, by bolting trunnions to the sides near the center of gravity, was considered, but abandoned. The method adopted was to arrange a sort of wooden hinge about which the shaft and casing were revolved while being raised to an upright position.

A twelve-inch timber three quarters round and one quarter square was fitted to the bottom stringer timbers at the end next the base of the monument. This was allowed to rest on other timbers which had been hollowed out half round. In erection, the whole of the shaft and casing rested on the round timber, which in turn rested on and turned in the timbers hollowed out to receive it.

When the shaft was raised to an upright position it was landed upon an upright stone post, two feet square, set in the center of the base several inches above the permanent position of the bottom of the shaft. This stone post was supported upon a bed of sand in a pocket formed in the base of the monument, and so arranged that by opening a gate valve the sand would flow out and so lower the post and the shaft above, forming what may be termed a sand-jack.

The shaft was raised to an upright position by a tackle of twenty ropes, ten sheaves eighteen inches in diameter being fastened to the top of the casing of the shaft as previously described. The fixed block was made up of eleven sheaves of the same size, and was fastened with six two-and-one-half-inch eye-bolts to a sixteen by eighteen inch hard pine timber reinforced on the top by an iron plate one inch thick and eighteen inches wide. This cross-head timber was suitably fastened to the top of a stage built of heavy timbers from the ground to a height convenient for handling the shaft and the surmounting stone work. On the front the stage was braced on either side by two twelve by twelve inch timbers, and in the opposite direction it was guyed from the top to two posts two hundred feet apart and two hundred and fifty feet back of the monument. It was at first planned to use a breast derrick instead of a stage for the erection of the shaft, and a derrick one hundred and three feet high was built and erected. During the winter previous to the erection of the monument it was wrecked in a high gale, and a stage substituted instead of building another derrick.

The rope used in the tackle for hoisting was a three-quarter inch crucible steel wire rope, and rated by the manufacturers at a breaking strain of thirty-six thousand pounds. The greatest strain on the single rope during the erection to a vertical position was, neglecting friction, four thousand pounds; and afterward, when the whole weight of the stone and casing was held for a short time while the position of the shaft was being adjusted, the strain was slightly over nine thousand pounds.

Previous to the erection the shaft and casing were blocked up to as high an angle as was practicable and a trial lift made.

This trial developed a weakness in the front brace timbers, which was remedied by adding more guys to the back. When the final lift was made, everything worked smoothly, and in ten minutes the shaft was erect and resting on the stone post.

The cut (VIII) is a copy of a photograph taken while the shaft was being raised to an upright position.

It was intended to land the shaft on the stone post in the correct position for lowering on to the base; but, owing to a slight movement of the shaft in the casing, this was not accomplished. The correct adjustment was made by taking a strain on the lifting tackle, then locking the drums of the hoisting engine and allowing sufficient sand to flow out from under the stone to clear it from the whole weight of the shaft and casing. The shaft was then lashed in correct position and lowered back on the stone post. It will be noted that by this operation, while the whole weight was held for a given time, a direct lift was avoided.

When everything was ready for lowering the shaft to its final position the bottom part of the casing was sawed off and removed. The valve controlling the sand was then opened, and the running out of the sand allowed the shaft to settle gradually and smoothly to its permanent bed, which had previously received a thin layer of cement mortar. The bottom of the pocket for the sand was made conical in shape, it being found necessary by experiment in order to make the sand flow out uniformly. After the shaft was landed upon the stone post it was found to have compressed the sand three eighths of an inch, or two hundred and sixteen cubic inches in a total volume of sixteen cubic feet, under a direct compression of about three hundred and twelve pounds per square inch.